PRESERVE US A NATION

Renewing the American Character

Restoring the American Soul

Reviving the American Heart

CHARLES CRISMIER

Vision H
G

D1512090

*The arteries serving
the heart of America
are nearing total blockage
from the accumulated sludge
of moral relativism
over the last two generations.
Now America lies
in acute distress,
gasping for the oxygen of faith
and a flow of moral truth
that will restore her character
and revive her heart.
This book is open-heart surgery.
It is must reading for you,
your family,
and anyone who loves our land.
Its message is essential to
the survival of America.*

CONTENTS

PREFACE

Something Has Gone Wrong

THIS BOOK IS FOR *EVERY* American. We all come from differing nationalities, differing origins, and have differing perspectives. But one thing is nearly universal. We share a sense that something has gone wrong—that somehow we, as a nation, have gotten off track. How did it happen? Why did it happen? What can we do about it?

Prepare to Be Provoked

This book is intended to provoke your mind and stir your heart. If it does, and the flame of freedom and truth is re-ignited in your heart, it will have been worth the hours invested in its writing. One thing is certain: If we continue asking ourselves what went wrong and looking to "the other guy" to fix it, in a few short years this great American house will be beyond repair. But for now, repair is in order. We can do it because we care. We care about the future. We care about our children and our grandchildren. We care about America.

Join with me now as we inspect the damage and then get about the repair of this great American "house." Let's *"Preserve Us a Nation."*

The Issue Is Character

WE HAVE BEEN TOLD IN recent elections that "character" is irrelevant. In fact, many of us bought that message. The reason we so easily bought that message is that we have in many ways come to believe it ourselves. This is difficult to admit, isn't it? In our hearts, we don't want to believe this of ourselves. After all, America was built on character; it has been part of our identity. But we need only look around us to see the erosion and decay in that character—and its devastating consequences.

Problems have erupted—social problems, economic problems, gangs, violence, family breakdown, sexual perversion, fear—and we've begun to focus on these problems. They become more severe and out of control daily. Yet in reality, the things that demand our attention as the "problems" are only symptoms, and the root problem is seldom identified. So we wring our hands and try not to be afraid. We try not to think about where things really are headed—much less where we will end up.

There is a free-floating national anxiety. Many are on the edge of despair. We will look almost anywhere for hope. We have lost the big picture. We need *hope*...a hope based on something of substance, a hope upon which we can build a life and rebuild our nation.

America's Only Hope

The real issue *is* "character" which issues out of our moral fiber and our spiritual being. It is so fundamental that we have overlooked it. But we can no longer afford to avoid it. Together let us shift focus from the symptoms of our personal and national pain to solutions that will restore personal and national promise. It is America's only hope.

In this hour of crisis:
What I CAN DO is first defined
by what I SHOULD BE!

CHAPTER ONE

If I Could Speak

I WAS BUT A GLEAM in the eye of my father. He was attending a dinner party at the estate of Edouard de Laboulaye in Versailles, France. The year was 1865. Gathered there were a group of Frenchmen, and Laboulaye began excitedly expounding on his favorite subject—the United States of America.

A TALE OF TWO NATIONS

France and the United States had each gone through a revolution at nearly the same time—near the end of the 1700s. America had claimed her independence from Britain. Many, if not most, of the American colonists had preferred to remain loyal subjects of the British Crown, but abuses of power by King George III and increasing taxation without representation by the British Parliament finally turned the hearts of the American colonists to declare their independence. France had lent support to the American cause, especially by the hand of the celebrated Marquis de Lafayette.

The citizens of France had revolted against their own government just after the American Revolution. But the French Revolution was a much bloodier affair. They had fought against and among themselves. The French monarchy was abolished. King Louis XVI and his queen, Marie Antoinette, were beheaded by guillotine, along with thousands of their followers. Then the revolutionaries themselves struggled for power and executed each other. The blade of the guillotine never seemed satisfied with the blood that flowed. This period came to be known as the "Reign of Terror." Naturally there were sympathies among many of the American colonists for the French in their pursuit of liberty. But there were great fears as well, for while there were similarities, there was also something distinctly different underlying the two revolutions.

The French citizenry had been stirred and motivated by the writings and spirit of Voltaire and Rousseau, renowned philosophers of the day. It was the "Age of Enlightenment," or so they said. Frenchmen were being urged to repudiate all ties of society that might restrict or constrain—especially faith and family. "Enlightenment" thinking conveyed the idea that true freedom was liberation from God and from moral constraint, that there was no absolute truth, and that all truth was relative to the individual or group as they might enter into social compact together.

The American colonists, on the other hand, also pursued freedom, but they saw true freedom as voluntarily coming under the authority of Almighty God and His commandments as the Great Ruler of Nations. They found true liberty to issue from voluntary submission to law based upon the Bible as the authoritative Word of God. They had grappled with "enlightenment" philosophy and had largely rejected it.

AS A NATION THINKETH...

The American "experiment" in self-government had become an obvious success to the rest of the world. There was growth, excitement, and a clear sense of direction and purpose. France had not fared as well, and that was also quite obvious. She was unable to establish a stable government and had continuous internal problems, possessing a stunted sense of direction and purpose. And so it was in the 1830s that the French "sociologist," Alexis de Tocqueville, came to America to explore and study "the secret of her genius and power."

Several years of careful observation brought de Tocqueville to the conclusion that, "America is great because America is good." He recorded his findings in his book, *Democracy in America*. America's thinking had made a difference. Her

16

philosophy of life had determined her direction. And her thinking had been based on a faith that defined the behavior of her citizens. She was liberty in action. So de Tocqueville recorded, "Not until I went into the churches of America and heard her pulpits flame with righteousness did I understand the secret of her genius and power." The "American Dream" had been born. It was conceived in liberty, a special kind of liberty which carried her through a Civil War so that all of her people might enjoy the blessings of liberty. America had become a beacon light to the world.

CONCEIVED IN LIBERTY

My father was an artist—a sculptor. At the age of thirty-one, he had become renowned as a builder of patriotic statues. As he sat with his friend Laboulaye following dinner in that Versailles palace, talk turned to the desire for a republican form of government in France. There was a feeling of kinship among the French as they watched American liberty blossom. As the men talked, Laboulaye suggested giving a giant statue to the United States to unite the two countries in the cause of liberty. This is how I was conceived in the mind of my father, Frederic Auguste Bartholdi, who had never even been to America.

In August of 1871, my father set off on a trip across America to generate interest in my birth. He was amazed and nearly overwhelmed by the vastness of the land and the wonder of her beauty. After five months, he had spread word of his plans. His enthusiasm was never dampened, though no one offered to help pay for the project. And he named me before I was born: "Liberty Enlightening the World."

BIRTH OF A LADY

He determined I should be a lady. I was to hold the torch of freedom high. But France was still in a state of political turmoil. Finally, in 1874, when the French Assembly completed a written constitution for the Third Republic, my father decided the timing was right to publicly present to his countrymen his idea that France give a monument of liberty to the United States.

His goal was to raise $250,000 for my birth, scheduled for July 4, 1876. Fund-raising was time consuming. He had built a four-foot tall-model of a dignified lady draped in a classic Roman gown. Her face was grim in her determination to rise victorious over all forms of tyranny, holding high the torch of freedom. Her sandaled feet had broken the chains of oppression. She wore a crown of seven spikes, representing the seven seas and seven continents. This is what I was to become.

I don't have time to describe in detail all the joys and sorrows which attended my birth. A steel framework was erected by Gustave Eiffel, the famous engineer of Eiffel Tower fame. I was given a thin copper skin. Effort was made to prevent galvanic corrosion by insulating my iron framework and supports from contact with my copper skin. Six hundred thousand rivets bound my skin to my skeleton. After my pedestal had been built in America, I was shipped in 214 crates to be assembled on-site. On October 28, 1886, I was born on Bedloes' Island in New York Harbor amidst much fanfare. At birth I stood three hundred five feet and one inch from foundation to torch, and weighed two hundred twenty-five tons.

GROWING PAINS

I was thrilled as I stood high over New York Harbor. I watched American merchants transport their goods to other nations. I reveled in the hustle and bustle of people and progress. I felt almost as if I stood watch over the handiwork of God Himself as the nation recovered from the Civil War and prospered, seemingly in the favor of God and man across the world.

When I was born, many rejoiced—but some jeered. Some felt that perhaps I would be a pagan influence. But that was never my intent or in my heart. I knew I was, deep down, only a symbol, and that true liberty was born, not in the heart of man, but in the heart of God. It was clear that man, made in the image of God and following Him, experienced that same spirit of liberty, for it was written, "Where the Spirit of the Lord is, there is liberty" (2 Corinthians 3:17).

I witnessed the fervent spirit of many Americans. They were a God-fearing people who clearly found their roots in the Bible. While some did not espouse Christian faith, most did, and all were convinced that the only workable guidelines for life, business, and self-government were to be found in the Bible. And so the Bible was the basis for our laws, our families, and our society together.

In fact, just six years after I was born, our United States Supreme Court, in a case referred to as *The Church of the Holy Trinity vs. United States*, declared, "...this is a Christian nation." This America in which I was born was *good*...not perfect, but very good. It was a joy to be among the people. That the nation was blessed by the hand of God was beyond dispute. And the joy of that goodness and the prosperity it brought caused me to glow from the inside. I felt like radiating the light of that blessing across the seas and the continents, for there was great suffering and discontent elsewhere in the world. Although I had a few skin and minor skeletal problems in those day, I felt good. It was good to be here.

THE LIGHT THAT SHINES

It has been said that beauty is only skin deep. But the beauty of America was not just what one could see, it was what one could *feel*. It was as if it went to the core of her very being...to her heart. So I felt the essence of her moral goodness in my heart. And I was not alone. It was as if America was the very essence of goodness, of life, of purity, of nobility of mind and purpose. I felt this myself. And as I stood welcoming those following my beacon light to safe harbor on these shores, it was clear I had become not only a symbol of liberty, but of moral goodness and virtue as well. I believe true liberty should breed virtue...and it did.

People flooded by me daily in ships from around the world. It was a never-ending procession. But they did not come to visit; they came to stay. They fled persecution, corruption, violence, and poverty. They yearned to be free and to experience the blessings of liberty in a land of opportunity...in a land where God presided as Lord over the affairs of men. We could hardly keep up with the teeming masses following the light of liberty. As my father had said when he named me, I was indeed "Liberty Enlightening the World."

A MOTHERING HAND

Interestingly, my role in symbolizing liberty was not yet clearly established. It takes time to become accepted and recognized. But when people need you, it's amazing what can happen in their thinking.

The world was becoming more intense. Storm clouds of war darkened the horizon. Suddenly we found ourselves involved in "the war to end all wars"—World War I. I was concerned along with the rest of the American people. Although the battle did not rage on our shores, there was fear. We even had a surprise attack on a munitions facility across the bay from where I stood. These were *real* fireworks, and I was wounded by the explosions. Fortunately, my injuries were not serious.

Our people needed a rallying point. Liberty was at stake. We had to pull together, not only for ourselves but for peoples around the world. They looked to us. And Americans began to look to *me*. I stirred the hearts of my countrymen. I held the torch of freedom high and was finally accepted by America. I was no longer just a mother to tired immigrants but a source of encouragement to the nation. People began calling me "The Statue of Liberty." My mothering hand of freedom was held high to all.

YEARS OF LEAN, YEARS OF PLENTY

The war was over. We thought we had made the world safe for democracy. It was not long, however, before we languished in a severe depression. We tried to hold our heads high while we stood in bread lines. By God's grace we recovered, but then came a second world war. It was tough. The price of freedom was not just vigilance but blood...the blood of our young men. We learned that freedom is not free. We paid the price. We sacrificed. And we were proud to keep our honor clean as we set about helping peoples around the world rebuild following our victory.

Victory is sweet, but prosperity in peace seems sweeter. I thrilled to see "swords beaten into plowshares." We began to feel good again; we prospered. And I had been there for my countrymen when they needed me as a symbol, and needed my encouragement and strength.

While I rejoiced in the blessings of liberty enjoyed by my countrymen, I was beginning to feel a bit ignored. It had been years since I received any personal attention. I had aided the cause of freedom as we fought—sometimes it seemed I was even the center of attention. But my skin was not fairing well. I began feeling aches and pains throughout my support skeleton. I tried to ignore the pains; I knew there was no time, no energy, nor money for maintenance and repair. But I was beginning to weaken. The stress of the harsh living environment was corroding my inner being. Yet I received only token attention to my needs.

How could this be, amidst such prosperity? I thought. *Surely there is sufficient time now to attend to my maintenance. We are no longer at war. Surely there are adequate finances to keep me in repair.* A few seemed concerned, but most went on about their business. I tried not to worry or think about the increasing feelings of weakness in my body. I felt it reaching increasingly into the very heart of my being. *And this is prosperity?* I thought.

LIKE MOTHER, LIKE DAUGHTER

My thoughts began to wander. With every pain I felt in my iron bones, I began to consider the well-being of the nation I had served. With every cry of my inner being, I sensed a cry from the hearts of my countrymen. I had become like a mother to my countrymen. And as I looked at my tattered skin in the light reflecting from the waves of life crashing about me, I saw also the darkened countenance and pitted image of the faces of the daughters of America. And then I realized the truth. *I am only a symbol. My countrymen are the substance.*

And what was happening to me was also happening to them. They were being corroded from the inside out by the godless forces and humanistic philosophies that had torn the heart from the nation from which my father had come. America was weaker now, and without the vitality that had characterized her at her birth. And I saw the devastating effect of corrosion of inward character in the faces and lives of the countrymen I had come to love. I was grieved. It was "like mother, like daughter."

Finally some began to take my plight seriously. When they took the time from their busy schedules, they discovered that, not only was my copper skin in need of repair, severe corrosion in my foundation and framework threatened my very existence. I recalled the words of my father, Bartholdi. He had thought I would stand the test of time, that I would stand as a beacon of liberty for thousands of years. I would never fall. I had thought the same of America. But if something did not happen soon, my days were numbered. So I worried for America.

LIBERTY OR DEATH

I was dying. That was a terrible thought. I could hardly face it. But it was true. Careless use and abuse had left me unprepared for the pressures and trials of a new century...a new millennium. Yet I wanted to live. I wanted to continue to stand tall, to hold the torch of freedom high for the world and for the American people.

I saw and felt the agony of body and spirit wracking the lives of my fellow Americans. Thoughts rushed through my mind. How could this have happened? How could I, thought to be a timeless symbol, be in a life-and-death struggle? How could America, looked upon by her people and the world as a timeless bastion of freedom, be struggling with a cancerous corrosion of inner character and spirit that threatens her very existence? Yet I could not deny the truth. The carelessness of years of personal peace and affluence had allowed the very fiber of her being to be eaten way.

I turned away. It is hard to look at the ravages of cancer on a body. It is hard to accept the torn families, broken lives, violence, economic despair, and lack of sense of direction, meaning, and purpose that set in. But I saw it in the lives of my countrymen. And then I understood more clearly that, indeed, "the price of liberty is eternal vigilance." When the price is not paid, the price of eternal vigilance, a much higher price will be paid: the ultimate price, *death.* I could not bear the thought.

RESTORING THE SYMBOL

Then it came to me—*they are going to restore me.* America is not going to let me die. My countrymen are not going to allow internal corrosion to eat away my substance. They are rallying to the cause. They say it will be expensive, but that which is valuable *is* costly. Perhaps it would not be so if I had been attended to faithfully. But we cannot wish for what might have been. I am dying. It will take heroic measures to preserve me...and over two hundred fifty million dollars.

I also considered, *What will it take to preserve my nation?* It may take billions. Yet it is really not a matter of dollars and cents, for my countrymen are already spending themselves silly. No, my nation does not need money. She needs mothers and fathers who are committed to training their children. She needs school teachers who live lives of principle and are not afraid to impart the same. She needs husbands who love their wives and wives who respect and honor their husbands. She needs businessmen who will not lie. She needs lawyers who triumph only in the truth. She needs public servants and not politicians. She needs pastors and priests who will not pander for popularity among their parishioners by trading God's timeless truth for the tawdry self-interest of self-help doctrines. She needs men and women of character...of courage...and of compassion. She needs a new you and a new me.

So I was ecstatic when leaders among my countrymen committed to restoring me. It was not to be "skin deep." I heard them say they would renew, rebuild, and restore me from the inside out. And I hoped they would do the same for my nation...the land that I love.

It took several years. My iron ribs were replaced or repaired. New protection was provided to prevent the terrible corrosion that had eaten away my inward parts. Care was taken to protect against those who would attack my inward being with dark and perverted messages of modern philosophy through graffiti on the walls of my mind. My foundations were secured and my framework rebuilt, for the original design was good.

After my inner substance was restored, my copper skin was cleaned and my blemishes removed. I felt like a new woman. The work on the inside was reflected on the outside. I yearned for such a work for my America, but all I heard was the anguished cry of her people out of the pain of her decay. I was deeply grieved for her, desiring that she experience the same joy of restoration. But there seemed little interest among my countrymen. They seemed not to see the connection between my decay and theirs.

My crowning glory was the replacement of my beacon light and the torch of freedom. I was nearly overwhelmed with emotion. With body and soul again whole, my light of liberty once again shown even more brightly across the seas and continents of the world. Darkness had been creeping in. Moral decline and spiritual decay enshrouded my being with an ominous dusk that foretold the twilight of liberty...and even civilization itself.

One hundred years had brought me near death. Now, gloriously, as my beacon light of virtue and liberty blazed forth across the waters with renewed intensity on October 28, 1986, darkness was dispelled. I stood tall once again, secure that the blessings of liberty and the light of freedom were assured to generations to come. But then I painfully remembered—*I am but a symbol*. My mind was wrenched! I cried out from within: "Which way America? Which way will you go? This is my country, and I want to know. Which way, America, will you go?"

And I ask you, my countrymen, "Which way will you go?" I realized long ago that America is no greater than her people. Her faith is no greater than your faith. Her courage is no stronger than your courage. Her virtue is no purer than your virtue. Her principles are no firmer than your principles. Her vision is no clearer than your vision. Her foundation is no more secure than your foundation. Her heart is no more compassionate than your heart. And God's truth will only march on if it marches in your boots.

So which way will you go, father, mother, husband, wife, businessman, politician, pastor, priest? Will you ignore your corrosion of mind and heart? Will you wink at the corruption of your character? Will you pursue business as usual until your light is darkness and you have no more strength to stand? Or will you arise, rebuild, and once again restore the beacon light of freedom and the virtues of true liberty in your life, that government *of* the people, *by* the people, and *for* the people shall not perish from the earth?

As Lady Liberty, I cry out to you, my countrymen, with impassioned soul, "Preserve me a nation!" And to the great Ruler of Nations who governs in the affairs of men, I plead:

God bless America,
Land that I love;
Stand beside her,
And guide her,
Through the night

With the Light
From above;

From the mountains,
To the prairie,
To the ocean
White with foam,

God bless America,
My home, sweet home;
God bless America,
My home, sweet home.[1]

There is no national character
without personal character.

CHAPTER TWO

A Nation at Risk

IN HER RELATIVELY SHORT EXISTENCE, America has impacted the world for good like no other nation in history. From a fledgling association of thirteen colonies struggling to get up and walk as a nation of one people, to her position as the nation to which all eyes turn in the world, America has been blessed. One can scarcely indulge in even a brief review of her meteoric rise from the heroic bloodshed of her Revolutionary War to her position as leader among the powers of the earth without seeing the unmistakable hand of God upon her.

But America is at risk. Her foundations are cracking. The principles that made her great have become corrupted. Our character has become tarnished and our moral fiber is corroded. We are in turmoil from incessant infighting. We have become a nation where everyone is a minority striving for "special interests." There is no "common sense." But our enemy is not from without; our enemy is within us. There is a "civil war" raging in the hearts and minds of Americans. Can we survive? Can America be saved?

OUR CONSTITUTION WAS "SAVED"

As our Founding Fathers deliberated day after day in the seething heat of a Philadelphia summer to hammer out a

29

constitution that would serve the emerging nation, they met with nerve-wracking frustration as delegates from each colony sought to protect their special interests. Tempers flared. Passions were inflamed. The task of achieving any consensus for a workable plan for the new government seemed doomed. Some delegates had already walked out. At this moment of despair and seeming hopelessness, Benjamin Franklin, the elder statesman, rose and addressed the president of the convention, George Washington, and declared:

Mr. President,

In this situation of this Assembly, groping as it were in the dark to find political truth, and scarce able to distinguish it when presented to us, how has it happened, Sir, that we have not hitherto once thought of humbly applying to the Father of lights to illuminate our understanding! In the beginning of the contest with Great Britain, when we were sensible of danger, we had daily prayer in this room for the Divine protection. Our prayers, Sir, were heard, and they were graciously answered.... And have we forgotten this powerful Friend? Or do we imagine we no longer need His assistance? I have lived, Sir, a long time, and the longer I live, the more convincing proofs I see of this truth—that God governs in the affairs of men.

Benjamin Franklin then went on to declare to that awesome assembly of the greatest minds in America: "If a sparrow cannot fall to the ground without His notice, is it probable that an empire can rise without His aid?"

Then he declared: "We have been assured, Sir, in the Sacred Writings, that except the Lord build the house, they labor in vain that build it."

The senior statesman then delivered his personal conviction concerning the future of the nation:

I firmly believe that without His concurring aid, we shall succeed in this political building no better than the builders of Babel. We shall be divided by our little partial local interests; our projects will be confounded; and we ourselves shall become a reproach and a bye word down to future ages.... I therefore beg leave to move—that henceforth prayers imploring the assistance of Heaven, and its blessings on our deliberations, be held in this Assembly every morning before we proceed to business....[1]

The assembly of fifty-five of America's greatest intellects and leaders solemnly and humbly adopted Benjamin Franklin's motion, and each session was thereafter begun with prayer for God's guidance and wisdom. The effect on the convention was nothing short of miraculous. The hand of divine providence was clearly revealed as wisdom began to preside over wrath and consensus prevailed over confusion. The members of the assembly began to seek principle rather than personal position. A sense of order and direction emerged, resulting in the drafting and adoption of what leaders throughout the world have acknowledged as the greatest document ever crafted by the human mind. No constitution of any nation in the world has endured as has that divinely inspired document. In the words of James Madison, principal drafter of the Constitution and our fourth president, "Without the intervention of God there never would have been a Constitution."[2]

CHRISTIAN CONSENSUS AND AMERICA'S GREATNESS

The consensus of Christian faith as the foundation of America and her greatness is replete in virtually every fiber of the original fabric of the nation. All thirteen of the original state constitutions refer to Almighty God as the author of liberty or declare reliance upon the hand and mercy of Providence.[3] George Washington declared, "Of all the dispositions and habits that lead to political prosperity, religion and morality are indispensable supports...."[4]

A generation after the Constitution was adopted, when the French political observer, Alexis de Tocqueville, came to the United States in the mid-1800s to study the success of the nation, he was greatly moved by what he found. He had observed how France struggled after the French Revolution—enmeshed in the "Enlightenment," a secular humanist world view. In America, he found a nearly universal belief in the principles of the Bible as the basis for law and life. He wrote in his book, *Democracy in America*: "America is great because

America is good. And if America ever ceases to be good, America will cease to be great."[5]

OUR PAST GIVES FOCUS TO OUR FUTURE

Woodrow Wilson, the twenty-eighth president of the United States of America, expounded to us as a people: "A nation which does not remember what is was yesterday does not know what it is today, nor what it is trying to do."[6]

George Washington, our founding president and commander-in-chief of the American Revolution for Independence, gave us a legacy worth remembering. Simply stated in his farewell address: "Reason and experience both forbid us to expect that National morality can prevail in exclusion of religious principle."[7]

This legacy was confirmed and at the same time reiterated when we officially adopted as our national motto:

"In God We Trust."

Similarly, our flag salute was officially changed in 1954 by an act of Congress that we might be:

"One Nation *Under God*."[8]

But we have, in this last generation, forgotten the divine "Friend" whose power and guidance our forefathers relied upon. We have allowed the strident voices of a minority to convince us that our Creator should be dismissed from the halls of political debate, from the classrooms of our youth, from our decisions as a people, and from our conduct as individuals.

The shift from dependence upon our Maker to reliance upon ourselves has undermined the very foundations of America. The foundations are cracking and America is slipping off its foundation. Even secular observers now join in identifying the frightening picture before us. Witness some recent national headlines and commentaries:

"How Our American Dream Unraveled"[9]
—*Newsweek*, March 2, 1992

"The Glooming of America—A Nation Down in the Dumps"[10]
—*Newsweek*, January 13, 1992

"...We believed that prosperity would create the Good Society.
We were wrong."[11]
—*Newsweek*, March 2, 1992

"The Fraying of America"[12]
—*Time*, February 3, 1992

"If America doesn't watch out, it is going to be judged as finished by the world."[13]
—*Associated Press*, January 21, 1992

"Voters are demanding in their leaders the personal virtues they decreasingly demand of themselves."[14]
—*Time*, April 27, 1992

"We unwittingly adopted a view of human nature that assumed spiritual needs could ultimately be satisfied with material goods."[15]
—*Newsweek*, March 2, 1992

It is clear. If we want to save this great American "house," we must repair and rebuild the foundations. But when a great house has become so decayed that even its foundations lie in ruin, it becomes necessary to go back to the original building plans to determine how that house was built. Where and how were the foundations established? What building materials were used? In the following chapter we will inspect the "building plans" of America—the greatest national "house" perhaps in the history of mankind. We must rediscover her original foundations.

*A house with a
crumbling foundation
will soon be a crushing house.*

CHAPTER THREE

Remembering Our Foundations

No American president has ever enjoyed greater respect and honor for truth and integrity, as viewed through the eye of history, than Abraham Lincoln. President Lincoln clearly enunciated the source of America's blessing or that of any nation:

> "It is the duty of nations, as well as of men, to own their dependence upon the overruling power of God and to recognize the sublime truth announced in the Holy Scriptures and proven by all history, that those nations only are blessed whose God is the Lord."[1]

John Adams, second President of the United States, declared:

> "Our Constitution was made only for a moral and religious people. It is wholly inadequate to the government of any other.
>
> "We have no government armed with power capable of contending with human passions unbridled by morality and religion."[2]

CONSEQUENCES OF UNDERMINED FOUNDATIONS

For just a brief moment, let us take a fleeting glimpse at what we have become as a nation. How has this great house slipped? It's painful but we must look, for America's future, your future, and the future of your children may depend on it.

James Patterson and Peter Kim, advertising executives of the respected J. Walter Thompson Agency in New York, set out to take the "moral pulse" of America in the 1990s. Using state-of-the-art research techniques, they conducted the largest poll of private morals ever undertaken, to unearth the personal ethics, values, and beliefs of Americans of our time. Their findings are disclosed in a book every American who cares about his country should read: *The Day America Told the Truth*. The following are illustrative excerpts of their findings:

- America has no leaders and, especially, no moral leadership.
- Our void in leadership—moral and otherwise—has reached a critical stage. We still want leadership; we just can't seem to find it.
- There is absolutely no moral consensus at all in the 1990s.
- Americans are making up their own rules, their own laws, their own moral codes.
- Only thirteen percent of us believe in all of the Ten Commandments.
- Sixty percent of all Americans have been victims of a major crime. Fifty-eight percent of those people have been victimized twice.
- One in seven Americans has been sexually abused as a child.
- One in six Americans has been physically abused as a child.
- The number one cause of our business decline is low ethics by executives.
- While we still marry, we have lost faith in the institution of marriage.
- A majority of us will not take care of our parents in old age.
- Most Americans have no respect for what the law says.

- The Protestant ethic is long gone from today's American workplace.

- Every seventh person you pass on the street in America is carrying a weapon either on their person or in their car.

- America is "the most violent country in the world."

- Children's [television] programming now averages twenty-five violent acts per hour.

- Whether we are adults or children, the sheer volume of the violence we witness is numbing.... This urge toward violent action is creating real epidemics in America— epidemics of violence.

- Lying has become an integral part of the American culture, a trait of the American character.

- We can no longer tell right from wrong. It raises fear and doubt, which often leads to depression.

- Americans in the 1990s have more of both freedom and doubt—and of depression too—than did any previous generation.[3]

Patterson and Kim conclude:

- Americans wrestle with these questions in what often amounts to a moral vacuum. The religious figures and Scriptures that gave us rules for so many centuries, the political system that gave us our laws, all have lost their meaning in our moral imagination: We've become wishy-washy as a nation. Some would say we've lost our moral backbone.[4]

WHAT CAN WE DO?

A newspaper reporter attended a gathering where I spoke on the subject, "Stand Up America." I had conveyed much of the same information in that meeting as that which you have just read. The reporter called me at my office soon after and asked, "What can we do to save America? What do you want us to do?"

At first I was puzzled by his question because the answer seemed obvious. As we chatted, however, I quickly learned the answer was not obvious to him, nor is it obvious to the majority of my countrymen. We have slipped so far off our foundations that we have lost sight of and vision for truths and principles which formerly defined our very identity as a nation. Just as Woodrow Wilson warned, "Americans no longer remember what we were yesterday; therefore, we do not know who we are today or even what we are trying to do."

Thomas Jefferson, author of our Declaration of Independence, gives us direction in answering this threshold question, "What can we do to save America?" His voice still speaks, for the following words are inscribed on the Jefferson Memorial in our nation's capital:

God who gave us life gave us liberty. Can the liberties of a nation be secure when we have removed a conviction that these liberties are the gift of God?[5]

Jefferson is reminding America: If we want to continue to enjoy the liberties which our Founding Fathers secured at great cost, we must restore the conviction and acknowledge unashamedly that these liberties are the gift of God—not of ourselves—and then conduct our national and individual lives accordingly. We must return to the foundational principles of the Bible, the instruction manual of the Almighty for His creatures and creation.

Noah Webster, author of the oldest dictionary in America and a leading voice in the early development of our nation, could not more clearly set forth this essential element of our national prosperity. His statesmanship rings forth:

The moral principles and precepts contained in the Scriptures ought to form the basis of all our civil constitutions and laws. All the miseries and evils which men suffer from vice, crime, ambition, injustice, oppression, slavery, and war, proceed from their despising or neglecting the precepts contained in the Bible.[6]

Thomas Jefferson's words continue to reverberate:

Indeed I tremble for my country when I reflect that God is just, that His justice cannot sleep forever.[7]

I spent considerable time with that newspaper reporter, engaged in discussion about where we are as a nation and about the critical need to rebuild our moral and spiritual foundations. I told him we must turn the tide of public sentiment. His response reflects the mind and thought of many Americans. He said, "Mr. Crismier, that's a tall order. That could take years, a decade, maybe a generation!" To which I responded, "That's right! Rome was not built in a day, neither was it destroyed in a day."

We live in an "instant" society. We demand instant gratification, instant solutions. Our "button-pushing" mentality is a modern version of the fairy waving the magic wand. But the most valuable things in life do not come instantly or by magic wands: things such as faith, character, integrity—things worthy of building one's life on; things on which to build or rebuild a nation.

FROM THE PRINCIPLE TO THE PERSONAL

We cannot succeed if we do not begin. We must chart our course—a course to rebuild the moral and spiritual foundations of America. We must rebuild the American character. Begin *today!* Begin in your own life...in your family...wherever you are. Begin!

The short chapters which follow are intended to help us translate the basic need to rebuild the moral and spiritual foundations of America into practical, personal reality. It can be done! It will not be accomplished by the president, by Congress, or by any political process. It will be accomplished by you, by me, by your family, by my family, and by millions of Americans like you and me who love their country and pledge themselves to restore and preserve it.

THIS IS THE HOUR OF CRISIS!

Together, with God's help, we can change what *is* to what *should be*. We can become once again a nation of vision, of purpose, of character.

Together, we can SAVE AMERICA.... We can *PRESERVE US A NATION.*

> "If the foundations be destroyed,
> what can the righteous do?"[8]
> —*The Bible*

I must be what I should be
if I would do what I must do.

CHAPTER FOUR

America's Search for Leaders

THERE IS A NATIONAL CRY for leadership in America today. Why can't we find in this "enlightened" moment in our history men and women who challenge the hearts and minds of their countrymen? Why is there no sense of direction? Why is there waning hope and increasing despair? Where have all the leaders gone? In the next few pages, we will look briefly at qualities and characteristics which make for effective leaders. Dare to imagine being characterized by these qualities. But first, let's look once again to our Founding Fathers.

EXAMPLES FROM OUR FOUNDING FATHERS

After the American Revolution, and at about the time of the Constitutional Convention, the population of the thirteen colonies was approximately three million. That is nearly the size of Los Angeles today (the city, not the county). It was said by Thomas Jefferson of the fifty-five delegates who gathered at the Constitutional Convention in Philadelphia in 1789 that, "A more able assembly never sat in America."

Who would make such an observation of any gathering of "leadership" in Los Angeles, in Washington, D.C., or even in the entire nation today?

45

While our Founding Fathers did not all agree with one another on every issue, there was a camaraderie of respect and a recognition of the qualities of leadership among them. While they may not have manifested perfection in all of life's arenas, there was a perception generally that they were worthy of honor.

I have examined the lives of these men who laid the foundations for this great nation to see what made them men worthy of honor and respect—men who could not only lead but establish a nation. While they each had weaknesses, as a group they were:

An example of *VISION*;
An example of *PRINCIPLE*;
An example of *TRUTH*;
An example of *VIRTUE*;
An example of *HONOR*;
An example of *FIDELITY*;
An example of *COURAGE*;
An example of *RESPONSIBILITY*;
An example of *FAITH*;
An example of *COMPASSION*;
An example of *INTEGRITY*.

They were all, in their own way, *ambassadors for America*—for her goodness, for her greatness. You, too, can and will be a leader and an ambassador as you become, or continue to be, an example of these qualities.

TO BE A LEADER, I MUST FIRST BECOME A FOLLOWER

It is indeed strange that those who reach or strive for leadership find their path strewn with many sorrows, and constantly risk public rebuke and censorship. We seldom genuinely respect such a "leader." Although such people may gain temporary notoriety, they leave no lasting endearing memory in the hearts and minds of those who follow. We find such "leaders" in our businesses, churches, clubs, and government.

If a man is unwilling to submit to authority, he cannot rightfully expect others to submit responsibly to his authority. The insurgence of rebellion in the American culture has, therefore, severely impacted our ability to produce genuine leaders. I cannot harbor a rebellious spirit and develop righteous leadership.

James Madison, our third president and known as the "Father of the Constitution," alluded to this concept when he said:

Before any man can be considered as a member of Civil Society, he must be considered as a subject of the Governor of the Universe.[1]

Our growing refusal as a people to submit to the "Governor of the Universe" has manifested an upsurge in rebellion of spirit which has, in this last generation, severely frustrated our ability to produce true leadership. As a consequence, we are experiencing widespread disillusionment among the American people, not only with those who purport to lead but also with the institutions they head—whether in government, religion, education, or even law enforcement. Thus, for lack of trustworthy leadership, the framework of American society is threatening collapse.

No life in history has ever produced more followers than that of Jesus Christ. He submitted to authority and thereby gained authority. It is said in the Bible (Philippians 2:8) that Jesus first "humbled himself, and became obedient...." The result was that God "highly exalted him, giving him a name that was above every name: that at the name of Jesus, every knee should bow..."[2]

Virtually every one of our Founding Fathers bowed their knee to the Almighty as the "Governor of the Universe," and were not ashamed to do it. The greatest nation on earth was born as a result, and those founders were exalted. We continue to reap their blessings today. Will you be a leader in America? Have you bowed your knee? If not, I urge you to take that first step. You *will* become a leader in your home, on the job, in your community. For he who humbles himself before his Maker will be exalted.

LEADERSHIP IS ACTING ON WHAT I BELIEVE

Leadership is acting on what you believe. After you have acted, those around you will ascribe to you the title of "leader."

The brave men who in signing the Declaration of Independence pledged "their lives, their fortunes, and their sacred honor" to establish liberty and justice, did so not to

47

perform a mere task but to carry out a principle, and for that they receive the tribute of "leader"—of "Founding Father."

If we wish to *save America*, we must *act* on what we believe.

LEADERSHIP IS NOT SOMETHING I HAVE BUT SOMETHING I DO

Leaders are grown, not born. Leadership can be developed. *You* can develop leadership. Yes, you can be a leader. The greatest leader is not one who can lead millions but one who can lead his own family.

America needs your leadership!

I honor the example of my father. He came from simple stock. Bashful by nature and not endowed with much of this world's goods, he served for fifty years as pastor of small congregations across America—leading, encouraging, and guiding to preserve the "stuff of life"—true moral and spiritual values. At nearly eighty years of age, he continues to serve, now as chaplain for a major hospital.

I give tribute to my father-in-law as well. As a railroad man and blue-collar worker for all of his working years, he never saw himself as having that leadership "something" to offer. A few years ago, he moved to a small desert community, and it has been refreshing to see his life blossom with the leadership of serving in a small desert church.

TO BECOME A LEADER, BECOME A SERVANT

America was built on selfless service. Our ability to serve is rooted in our character—in the moral and spiritual fiber of our being—both individually and as a nation. The moral and spiritual decay in our land has infected both our national character and our individual character, resulting in a perversion of true service. The principled motivation for "public service" which we admire in our Founding Fathers has, in large measure, degenerated in this generation to "service" motivated by avarice and personal gain.

Service is the highest form of leadership! The greatest Leader in history tells us in the Scriptures, "He that is greatest among you shall be your servant" (Matthew 23:11). Of the fifty-six men who endorsed their names to the Declaration of

Independence, pledging their lives, their fortunes, and their sacred honor in service to their country, fourteen lost their lives in the cause, most lost their fortunes, but none lost their honor through the eye of history.

Undoubtedly the most memorable words spoken by John Fitzgerald Kennedy, our thirty-fifth president, were these:

Ask is not what your country can do for you—ask what you can do for your country.[3]

America needs leaders! Where can you serve? Find your niche *today*. America is depending on you.

A LEADER IS AN EXAMPLE

The wise Benjamin Franklin said, "None preaches better than the ant, and she says nothing." Many of us find it easier to "talk the talk rather than walk the walk." It seems easier to complain about the way things are than to do anything about it. It has become the great American pastime to accuse the president, bellyache about Congress, and chastise the governor. But where do *I* fit in? Where do *you* fit in? If I am unhappy about things or want change, can't I, *shouldn't* I, then set an example of what I expect?

Albert Schweitzer said, "Example is not the main thing in life—it is the only thing."[4] Seneca told us, "Noble examples stir us up to noble actions."[5] Certainly we share a rich heritage of noble examples from our forefathers, examples of:

Personal Responsibility
Honesty
Integrity
Honor
Fidelity
Courage
Faith
Vision

Those examples stir us, encourage us, and as Emerson said, "lift us to higher ground."[6]

A few years ago, an incident occurred which forever impressed upon me the significance of the voice of example in leadership. A man whom I had not seen for many years called me at my office and asked me to lunch. I had no clue as to his purpose, other than renewal of friendship. After arriving at a local restaurant and a few minutes of social banter, he suddenly changed the conversation and said, "Chuck, I have a serious personal problem and need to talk to someone I can trust." He then went on, "I want to tell you why I have come to you." He then went on to relate a seemingly obscure incident that had occurred about seven years earlier.

We had been together with a group of people attending a large seminar. We had broken for lunch and were returning for the afternoon session, walking briskly. As we approached the crosswalk at the intersection, the "Don't Walk" light flashed on. My friend recounted for me, "You refused to cross against the light while the rest of us crossed, and I have never forgotten that. It made such an impression on me." I thought to myself, *Wow, someone is watching everything I do, hearing everything I say.*

But Someone is watching everything *you* do as well, and hearing what *you* say. The responsibility is awesome—but real. It is the essence of leadership. Those watching may be:

> your spouse,
>> your children,
>>> your co-worker,
>>>> your neighbor,
>>>>> your parishioner,
>>>>>> your constituent.

Leadership is often established in the "little" things. It is destroyed by inconsistency and the double standard. In a *Time* article entitled, "In Praise of Mass Hypocrisy," the writer pointed out, "As voters we profess shock that our candidates should behave as we do. The paradox is striking. Voters are demanding in their leaders the personal virtues that they decreasingly demand of themselves. There is a word for the profession of virtue accompanied by practice of vice—hypocrisy."[7]

Lest I personally should have fallen into pride over doing something right, I was deeply grieved when, not long after having lunch with my friend and hearing his praise for my trustworthiness, I received another call from a fellow attorney and friend. He began the conversation by asking, "Chuck, how did you enjoy your jaywalk across Lake Avenue this afternoon?" I was embarrassed, not only because my friend had both seen my action and identified it for what it was, but because it instantly brought to mind the prior incident where I had done right and had been a source of uplift. I didn't know my attorney friend was driving by at that moment as I pondered whether or not to jaywalk. But eyes *were* watching. I grieved inwardly because of my own wrong choice—but even more because of its potential impact on others.

Now, you may be thinking, "That's ridiculous! People do it all the time," or "That's just a little thing. Let's get serious and talk about something important." But let me remind you, "It's the little foxes that spoil the vine."

The leadership of America rests in my example. The leadership of America rests in *your* example, too—in the little things. Virtue was once a keynote word describing the American character. Have we lost contact with its meaning? I am responsible for my example...and its consequences. It is my greatest, most enduring *act* of leadership.

If America's future depends on your example, what is America's future?

May God bless America through your example, and through mine.

There is no national vision without personal vision.

CHAPTER FIVE

Restoring the American Vision

VISION IS THE CHOICE TO see beyond today and the power to create tomorrow. It is available to every American.

Can you see beyond today? Have the pressures and intensity of life enshrouded you as might a dense fog, causing you to focus from day to day only on those things immediately pressing about you?

Life has become increasingly intense in America, hasn't it? This generation has experienced more technological advances than the sum total of all advances preceding in the history of the world. Yet amidst these advances, as a people we find ourselves engulfed by stress that threatens to destroy the very beings technology purports to serve.

As a lawyer for many years, I have observed the gradual increase of stress and anxiety in the lives of the people I have served, and throughout American culture in general. It has been revealed in the attitudes, heart, and behavior of people toward each other:

of husbands to wives,
> of wives to husbands,
>> of parents to children,
>>> of children to parents;

of neighbor to neighbor,
    of friend to friend,
        of employer to employee,
            of employee to employer;
of parishioner to his pastor, priest, rabbi,
    of pastor, priest, and rabbi to parishioner,
        of citizen to his government,
            of government to its citizens;
of a man to himself,
    of a man to society,
        of society to a man;
of a man to the world,
    of the world to a man,
        of a man to his nation,
            of a nation to its people;
of a man to his God.

We have become, as a people, increasingly *"today"* oriented. At the same time, we have become increasingly *"self"* oriented. The two most characteristic questions reflecting the "vision" of American society at this moment in our history are:

"What's in it for *me?*"

    and

"What's it going to do for me *today?*"

In substance, we as Americans have lost our ability to see beyond today. *We have little or no vision for tomorrow.* And we have and are reaping the agonizing consequences of lack of vision.

DEMISE OF THE AMERICAN DREAM

The demise of the American Dream has little to do with economics at its root—but has everything to do with *VISION*.

America is suffering. We all know it. We know it because *we* are suffering. We feel it. We see it. It seems to be everywhere.

Our national magazines feature headlines like these:

"How Our American Dream Unraveled"
"The Glooming of America—A Nation Down in the Dumps"
"The Fraying of America"

We cannot escape it. You cannot escape it. Our American Dream is unraveling.

LIFE WITHOUT VISION

In the midst of our national agony and frustration we look for scapegoats. We point to the economy; we point to education; we point to crime; we point to dishonesty in business, government, religion, and even law enforcement; we point to lack of leadership.

We think privately and out loud:

"If only the economy were stronger..."

"If only we had more jobs..."

"If only we had more money for education..."

"If only we had stronger penalties for crime..."

"If only we had more honest politicians..."

"If only we had more honest businessmen..."

"If only we had more honest religious leaders..."

"If only we had more honest policemen..."

"If only we had some real leadership..."

I have only one response. If we are morally and intellectually honest with ourselves, we should be crying:

"If only we had not lost our *VISION*..."

Over a period of several years, my wife's eyes became clouded with cataracts. Simple tasks became more difficult. Her enjoyment of life decreased. Frustration and irritation mounted. But thanks to laser surgery, clear vision was restored, and so was my wife's quality of life.

Without vision, the quality of life in America has diminished as well. We are becoming increasingly frustrated and irritated with day-to-day life. We need moral and spiritual laser surgery to restore our vision. My wife had to become sufficiently desperate in her lack of vision to seek out and submit to the necessary surgery to correct the problem. Are we sufficiently desperate yet that we will seek that which will clear our personal and national vision?

As Americans, we have learned to focus on the symptoms of our disease rather than on the disease itself. It's easier this way...at least for *today*. If I focus on symptoms, I can cast the blame on the president, the governor, the school, the police department, the courts, the pastor, my parents, or the members of congress. I can absolve myself of responsibility.

As we all absolve ourselves individually and collectively of responsibility, *no one takes responsibility.* If no one takes responsibility, the nation and our entire culture collapses from within. Demoralization, anger, and frustration breed more of the same. The nation crumples due to the vacuity of vision and lack of leadership.

THE SEARCH FOR LEADERSHIP

The most debilitating consequence of loss of vision is loss of leadership. There is no true leadership without *vision.* Outside of the importance of personal example, vision is the single most important ingredient for genuine leadership. A nation that loses its vision loses its leadership. America has lost its vision, and America has lost its leadership.

Perhaps we can now better understand why we face such a national malaise and cannot seem to get a sense of direction. As we are told in Patterson and Kim's *The Day America Told the Truth*:

America has no leaders and, especially, no moral leadership.[1]

Our void in leadership—moral and otherwise—has reached a critical stage. We still want leadership; we just can't seem to find it.[2]

The unfortunate conclusion is that we will never see true leadership restored in America until we restore a vision for America. This should not come as a surprise, however, for God Himself has warned us in His Holy Word, "Where there is no vision, the people perish..."[3]

HOW IS YOUR VISION?

America has been unique among nations. Her uniqueness was in her vision and in her people. Abraham Lincoln declared that ours was a nation and government "of the *people*, by the *people*, and for the *people*."[4] This means America's vision is not established or maintained by a king, dictator, or president, but by her people—by you...and by me.

America has not lost her vision because we have lacked leadership. Rather, America has lost her vision because you and I have lost our vision.

What was the American *VISION?* What was it that enabled the early settlers to overcome seemingly insurmountable difficulties against odds that would totally deter the majority of us today? Why were they able to persevere? Was there a cause? To what heritage of vision do we owe our dutiful respect and attention, both in appreciation for the blessings of liberty we enjoy and in seeking to restore our national sight? How did our vision become tainted? How did we develop the cataracts that now impair our vision?

THE AMERICAN VISION

James Russell Lowell was asked by the French historian Francois Guizot, "How long will the American republic endure?" He wisely replied, "As long as the ideas of the men who founded it continue to dominate."[5] So what were the ideas of our Founding Fathers? What was their vision for America?

You probably would not welcome an exhaustive discourse on the entire scope of the vision of our Founding Fathers. Nor is such a thorough discussion necessary for our purposes here. But we do need to understand where we have been in order to comprehend where we are going as a nation. Let's take a brief look back to the very words of our Founding Fathers—as found in their letters, speeches, and other documents—for a summary of the unusual vision they shared for America.

Christopher Columbus

While Christopher Columbus was not actually a Founding Father of America, he has been credited, as an adventurer and explorer, for paving the way to the New World over one hundred years before the first settlers arrived on the eastern seaboard. He was convinced that God had given him a special responsibility to carry the light of Christ to heathen lands. His own name, *Christopher,* literally meant "Christ-bearer," and he believed this was additional confirmation of his call.

In his journal, Columbus, quoting the Book of Isaiah in the Bible, stated, "Listen to me, O coastlands, and hearken, you peoples from afar. The Lord called me from my mother's womb, from the body of my mother he named my name.... I will give you as a light to the nations, that my salvation may reach to the end of the earth."[6]

On each island where Columbus stopped, he instructed his men to erect a large wooden cross which he declared was "a token of Jesus Christ our Lord, and in honor of the Christian faith."

Unfortunately, as with most men, greed, gold, and glory clouded his own vision, and he eventually lost sight of the very life impetus which inspired and led him. His gradual loss of vision had profound negative impact, both on the motivations of those who would attempt to come to the New World for a century following, and in the ultimate loss of his own mind and personal integrity.

William Brewster

As an elder among the Pilgrims who, amidst untold persecution, had separated themselves from the Church of England, William Brewster gives poignant insight into the very heart and mind of those who would sail in 1620 for America and settle at Plymouth Rock. In a letter to the treasurer of the Virginia Company seeking financial backing for their enterprise, Brewster sets forth their reasons:

> We verily believe and trust the Lord is with us, unto Whom and Whose service we have given ourselves in many trials, and that He will graciously prosper our endeavors....
>
> We are knit together as a body in a most strict and sacred bond and covenant of the Lord....[7]

The Mayflower Compact

As the Pilgrims were preparing to land at Cape Cod on November 11, 1620, they drafted a simple compact which expressed their thoughts and intents for the new colony, as to its purposes under God and its government with the consent of the governed—the cornerstone of the American democratic republic.

> In the name of God, amen. We whose names are underwritten.... Having undertaken, for the glory of God and advancement of the Christian Faith and honor of our

King and country, a voyage to plant the first colony in the northern parts of Virginia, do by these presents solemnly and mutually in the presence of God and one another, covenant and combine ourselves into a civil body politic...[8]

William Bradford

William Bradford, Governor of the Plymouth colony from the time of the Pilgrims' landing on these shores and for nearly thirty years, reflecting on their labors and on the implementation of their original vision, stated: "As one small candle may light a thousand, so the light kindled here has shown unto many, yea in some sort to our whole nation...."[9]

John Winthrop

John Winthrop, an attorney and Cambridge graduate, was a leader of the Puritan movement in England. His godly example, practical wisdom, and servant's spirit placed him in natural leadership of the Puritans as they embarked to establish a colony at Salem.

Before the Puritans set foot on shore, Winthrop penned his clear vision for the colony which he entitled:

A Model of Christian Charity

We are a company, professing ourselves fellow members of Christ, we ought to account ourselves knit together by this bond of love....

Thus stands the cause between God and us: we are entered into covenant with Him for this work. We have taken out a Commission; the Lord hath given us leave to draw our own articles.... If the Lord shall please to hear us, and bring us in peace to the place we desire, then hath He ratified this Covenant and sealed our Commission.... But if we neglect the observance of these Articles...the Lord will surely break out in wrath against us.[10]

Winthrop understood that the vision was useless without corresponding action. He also knew the vision must be translated into the example of godly leadership.

Winthrop further sharpened his vision for the Puritan colony, saying the colony would stand as an example for others that followed. "The Lord make us like New England," he declared, adding, "...we must consider that we shall be as a City upon a Hill...."[11]

So great was the impact of John Winthrop, not only on the Puritan colony but on the heart of the developing nation, that at least one nineteenth-century historian ranked him second only to George Washington among the Founding Fathers.[12] Interestingly, there is a resurgence of interest among both secular and religious thinkers and writers suggesting that the only real hope for America is to restore the vision of John Winthrop.[13]

George Washington

The gentleman farmer from Virginia, George Washington, was urged by leaders of the colonies to become commander-in-chief of the Continental Army in our nation's fight for independence. After a bitter but victorious struggle with Great Britain, he was conscripted to chair the Constitutional Convention. So great was his respect and honor that he was said to be "first in the hearts of his countrymen."

As the first president of the United States of America, George Washington was keenly aware of the hand of God in establishing and preserving the new nation:

No people can be bound to acknowledge and adore the invisible hand, which conducts the Affairs of men, more than the People of the United States. Every step, by which they have advanced to the character of an independent nation, seems to have been distinguished by some token of a providential agency.[14]

Washington acknowledged the responsibility of the nation and its leadership to act only under the overruling authority of God:

Whereas it is the duty of nations to acknowledge the Providence of Almighty God, to obey His will, to be grateful for his benefits, to humbly implore His protection and favor....[15]

He understood and openly acknowledged before those who elected him to leadership that religious faith was a given essential to the health and prosperity of the nation and that they were so intertwined in the fabric of America as to be inseparable.

> Of all the dispositions and habits which lead to political prosperity, Religion and morality are indispensable supports.[16]

> Let us with caution indulge the supposition, that morality can be maintained without religion. Whatever may be conceded to the influence of refined education...forbid us to expect that National morality can prevail in exclusion of religious principle.[17]

In a farewell letter circulated to the governors of the thirteen states, Washington reaffirmed the covenant relationship of the American people to God and therefore of the people to each other.

> Almighty God; We make our earnest prayer that Thou wilt keep the United States in Thy Holy protection; and Thou wilt incline the hearts of the citizens to cultivate a spirit of subordination and obedience to government; and entertain a brotherly affection and love for one another and for their fellow citizens of the United States at large.

> And finally that Thou wilt most graciously be pleased to dispose us all to do justice, to love mercy, and to demean ourselves with that charity, humility, and pacific temper of mind which were the characteristics of the Divine Author of our blessed religion, and without a humble imitation of whose example in these things we can never hope to be a happy nation. Grant our supplication, we beseech Thee, through Jesus Christ our Lord. Amen.[18]

Benjamin Franklin

As the eldest statesman of the Constitutional Convention, Benjamin Franklin's wisdom was highly respected throughout the original thirteen colony states. After nearly five weeks of bickering and attacks among the fifty-five delegates, the vision for the rising nation and its spiritual moorings was shrouded in clouds of human passion. When all hope of a unifying Constitution seemed lost, Benjamin Franklin stood and, addressing President Washington, directed the attention of that great assembly to the God who had graciously protected the fledgling nation against staggering odds and whom they had ignored during weeks of deliberations.

> Have we now forgotten this powerful Friend? Or do we imagine we no longer need His assistance? ...The longer I live, the more convincing proofs I see of this truth—that God governs in the affairs of men.[19]

By his bold yet humble statesmanship, Franklin renewed the minds and hearts of his countrymen to the well-recognized covenant relationship the nation had enjoyed with Almighty God—the Hand of Providence. And upon their official recognition of this relationship, by beginning each day's deliberations thereafter with prayerful thanks and supplications for wisdom and guidance, God met His part of that covenant by bringing peace, wisdom, and a quality of thought that gave birth to the most effective national constitution ever drafted in the history of the world.

Franklin further expressed his vision for the relationship between freedom and the national character in declaring,

> "Only a virtuous people are capable of freedom."[20]

John Adams

John Adams, second president of the United States, continued the clear expression of the national vision and of the inextricable link between *faith* and *freedom,* as conceived in the fabric of that which is America.

> Our Constitution was made only for a moral and religious people. It is wholly inadequate to the government of any other.[21]

Thomas Jefferson

Thomas Jefferson, our third president, saw the signposts of slippage from the national vision. He knew the pride and selfishness of men's hearts and the threat these presented to the covenant between the people and their God and to the covenant between "We the people." He declared, "God Who gave us life gave us liberty."

He then issued a warning to echo down through every succeeding generation of Americans:

Can the liberties of a nation be secure when we have removed a conviction that these liberties are the gift of God?

Indeed I tremble for my country when I reflect that God is just, that His justice cannot sleep forever.[22]

IMPAIRED VISION

Many are indeed trembling in the land of the stars and stripes in the wake of the aimless, purposeless floundering of a ship of state that wallows in the consequences of impaired vision—without even a *sense* of leadership at the helm. Could it be that God's justice can no longer sleep? Could it be we have repudiated the very fountain of our national prosperity or the well-spring of the American character?

Have we developed cataracts in the American vision? Have we become blinded by generations of personal peace and affluence unparalleled in the history of the world, so that we can no longer see or discern the more fundamental issues of life itself—faith, truth, integrity, courage, compassion? If so, what can we do to restore vision in the land?

ONLY YOU CAN RESTORE VISION

Only *you*, with God's help, can restore vision. The president cannot do it. A different politician promising grandiose remedies and pandering to our pet concerns or needs cannot accomplish the task. We must knuckle under and face the truth. It will require changes in our lives, in the way we think, in our values, in the way we raise our children, in the way we spend our money and time—in our *hearts*. It will require "I" surgery.

We can and must make repairs and rebuild the foundations of our personal lives as Americans, in our families, in our businesses, in our churches, and in our government. But vision comes first. Without vision, we will become lost and even more frustrated in efforts to remedy, repair, and rebuild.

HOW YOU CAN RESTORE VISION

There are three basic ways you can restore vision in America. Each begins with you and me as individuals, and with our families.

FIRST: I MUST BRING TO PERSONAL REMEMBRANCE THE AMERICAN VISION.

Abraham Lincoln, at a moment of deep national crisis—a civil war that threatened to destroy the nation—found himself in a very lonely place in the White House. It is always lonely when leadership is required and vision is clouded or absent. In drafting his Gettysburg Address, at that desperate moment in our history, he reached back to a time when vision was clear as expressed in the lives of our Founding Fathers and in their writings which endure as our most precious heritage.

Lincoln distilled from those lives and writings which gave birth to the new nation an unmistakable truth and building block—the cornerstone of the American vision. He then redeclared on the battlefield of Gettysburg that truth which would restore and hold the vision of America for the century that followed:

This Nation, under God, shall have a new birth of freedom....[23]

My fellow Americans, voluntarily and humbly declaring our nation to be "under God" and then acting accordingly, is the sole and solitary prerequisite to restoring the American vision. New, believable, visionary leadership will then emerge. But America will never be "under God" unless you and I are "under God." In order to place ourselves "under God," we must choose to adopt God's ways, God's plans, and God's purposes as expressed in the Bible. We must repent or turn from our own pride, our rebellious ways, and our selfish ambitions, and choose to humble ourselves under God's hand. That must begin with those who profess to be Christian.

We are told in the Scriptures that if we will humble ourselves, the Almighty will exalt us; but if we exalt ourselves, we will be abased. Unfortunately, we are becoming more "abased" by the day. It is clear what we must do...and what we do, we must do quickly.

Our Forefathers knew that we would need to keep the vision ever before our eyes. The vision is declared from and is inscribed on every monument in our nation's capital:

In the Capitol Building

Preserve me, O God, for in Thee do I put my trust (Psalm 16:1).

In the Supreme Court

The Ten Commandments are inscribed over the head of the chief justice.

In the Library of Congress

What doth the Lord require of thee, but to do justly, and to love mercy, and to walk humbly with thy God (Micah 6:8).

In the Lincoln Memorial

As was said 3,000 years ago, so it must still be said, "The judgments of the Lord are true and righteous altogether."

In the Jefferson Memorial

Can the liberties of a nation be secure when we have removed the conviction that these liberties are the gift of God?

In the Congressional Building

In God we Trust.

May I ask you a personal question? Have you inscribed the American vision of a covenant relationship with God on the tablets of your own heart and mind? If not, do it today—for your sake, for your country's sake, and for the sake of your children.

SECOND: I MUST TEACH MY CHILDREN THE AMERICAN VISION.

Forbes magazine has been a foremost business publication on the American scene since 1917. Its seventy-fifth anniversary issue is dedicated to analyzing and responding to the grave sense of despair and anger in the land.

It declares, "It isn't the economic system that needs fixing. It's our value system."[24] Among the numerous articles in this issue, written by America's scholars and writers who are dedicated to exploring the nation's demoralized condition, are the following quotes from a single article:

Every parent in America knows that we're not doing a very good job of communicating to our children what America is and has been.[25]

We do not teach it as a society and we teach it insufficiently in our schools.[26]

Instead:

We teach the culture of resentment, of grievance, of victimization.[27]

We are certainly demoralizing our children....[28]

[In 1939] we could tell we were beginning to lose God—banishing him from the scene....[29]

And it is a terrible thing when people lose God.[30]

I don't think it is unconnected to the [baby] boomers' predicament that as a country we were losing God just as they were being born.[31]

It has been said that our children are a message we send to a world we will never see. What kind of a message are you and I sending through our children? What message have we failed to send?

If America's future depends on the vision for America which you have instilled in your children or grandchildren, what is America's future? We are writing America's future with every opportunity we fail to seize for the purpose of instructing and guiding the young lives entrusted to our care. They must be taught of the utter dependence of our Founding Fathers upon God's personal guidance and direction, both in their personal lives and in the building of the nation. Yes, we teach even when we fail to teach.

Teach your children well. America cannot survive another visionless generation.

THIRD: I MUST LIVE THE AMERICAN VISION.

None would deny the awesome truth that "actions speak louder than words." Yet we all find ourselves conducting our lives in ways that are hypocritical at one time or another. We can make excuses, we can conjure up every reason under the sun why we should be relieved of conforming to the standard of our verbal protestations of principle. But, over time, a telling story emerges from our behavior and attitude. We could call it a "life message."

So what is your life message? What message does our behavior and our attitude send to our children and grandchildren? What are we teaching them? What are we teaching them about what it *truly* means to be an American? Is what I am *really* teaching them the same message I want to leave them?

Based upon my example, what is the future of America? Do I want to face such a future? Would I want my children to face such a future? Most of us have been more concerned about living the American dream than the American vision.

Whether we like it or not, our day-to-day choices, decisions, behavior, and attitudes are defining or redefining the American vision for tomorrow. We are in crisis today because of our example yesterday—not just my example, not just the president's example, or that of the Congress—but *your* example, too.

Become an example of the American vision. And may God, through you, bless the America your children will inherit. As the Scriptures declare, "Blessed is the nation whose God is the Lord" (Psalm 33:12).

*I must sow what I should sow
if I would reap
what I should reap.*

CHAPTER SIX

A Matter of Principle

PRINCIPLES ARE LIKE SEEDS. If you don't plant them, utilize them, and live by them, they tend to blow away amidst the winds and storms of everyday living.

PRINCIPLES ARE FOR LIVING

As a lawyer for nearly two decades now, I have had both the pain and pleasure of working in the lives of thousands of individuals and families. I have sometimes seen my clients in their joys but usually in their sorrows. If there has been any common thread in their lives it has been this: A life or family without vision is usually a life or family without principles—and without principles, there is confusion, pain, heartaches, and destruction.

America's sage, Benjamin Franklin, reflected,

"If principle is good for anything, it is worth living up to."[1]

WHAT ARE PRINCIPLES?

So what are principles? How would I recognize a principle if I saw one? What are they for? How do they develop? What are the consequences of straying from principle? How can I become an example of principle in action? Let's explore the answers to these questions, for it is our answers to these questions that will guide us to restoring the American vision.

PRINCIPLES ARE SIGNPOSTS

Can you imagine traveling for any significant distance down a highway without having a signpost to give some assurance you are headed in the right direction?

I remember several years ago taking a trip with my family. As we drove along, we began to realize there were far fewer signs and indicators along the freeways in that region than we were accustomed to seeing. There was little warning of impending exits. Traffic was moving along at a vigorous clip and was unforgiving. We became increasingly frustrated as we searched for off-ramps to our destinations. The stress level in our vehicle was mounting and emotions became frayed.

Principles are life signposts. They point the way, provide order, prevent confusion, and give a sense of purpose. When the signposts of principle are absent or ignored, there is great frustration.

HOW CAN I KNOW A PRINCIPLE WHEN I SEE ONE?

Like a principle, a road sign will normally head you in a particular direction or give a specific life instruction. Principles can be broad or specific; they can give general direction or precise direction. They can also be "good" or "bad." Occasionally I have come across a road sign that gives incorrect or imprecise direction. You may have experienced the frustration of such "bad" road signs in your travels. They can lead to time-wasting detours and even prevent us from reaching our destination.

A "good" principle normally can be determined by how closely it compares to the following standards:

- Is it true in most every situation?
- Has it stood the test of time?
- Is it something I would want my neighbor to practice?
- Is it consistent with the plan of our Founding Fathers?
- Is it consistent in all respects with the plan of the Creator of all men, as shown in the Bible?

Failure of any principle to meet these tests should cause me to discard it, for my sake and that of my nation.

HOW HAVE WE STRAYED FROM PRINCIPLE?

Unfortunately, many of us as Americans have mistaken "pragmatism" for "principle." We have discarded the time-honored tests for principle upon which our nation was established and in their place we have substituted the tests of pragmatism: Is it expedient? Does it work for me? Does it work for me today? Which way is the wind blowing in my community, my school, my workplace, my church, my culture?

But in following the wind, we have reaped the whirlwind as a nation. We have ignored the principles of the ages in favor of the expedients of the hour.

THE CONSEQUENCES OF PRAGMATISM

America is in *CRISIS*! With those four words we began this book, and with them we define the consequences reaped from sowing seeds of pragmatism rather than principle. We have sown these seeds of expediency individually, as families, as businesses, as communities, and as a nation.

How did this happen? How could it happen? Thomas Jefferson warned us. He said, "Eternal vigilance is the price of liberty."[2] We have become slack. We went to sleep at our watch post over the last sixty years. We have not fallen into decay overnight. The blocks of our foundation have been eroded one at a time. It happened when we stopped measuring ourselves and our decisions, both individually and as a nation, by the yardstick of principles. Instead...

- we decided to turn over the care of the needy to the government rather than accept the responsibility ourselves;
- we decided to report only a portion of our actual income on our last tax return;
- we decided to ask for a "cash" payment rather than a check, so we "wouldn't have to report it";
- we decided to claim damage to our car that pre-existed an automobile accident in order to get insurance to repair it;
- we decided to "cheat" on our spouse;
- we decided to "call in sick" to our employer when we wanted to go shopping or vacationing;

- we made personal calls on the boss's time and tab;
- we fed our child from our plate at the all-you-can-eat salad bar;
- we loaded up our credit cards with purchases we couldn't afford to pay for;
- we printed more money to pay the national debt;
- we eliminated prayer and the Bible from our public education.

There are consequences which inevitably follow such choices. Let us look briefly at the cultural and social consequences that have devastated America as a result of our drift from principle to pragmatism in the last sixty years.

- We have a national debt of nearly four trillion dollars.
- We have a divorce rate that has more than tripled.
- Crime has escalated to the point that law enforcement can no longer keep up with it.
- Teenage pregnancy rates have soared.
- AIDS threatens to kill millions and consume billions.
- Homelessness is a national plague.
- Truth has nearly become extinct.
- We have greater wealth but more poverty of spirit.
- We have more counselors yet rampant depression.
- We have lost our sense of community.
- We use drugs and alcohol to deaden the reality of our choices.

We are not getting better. Education has not helped. We have never had so much "education." Education without principles, without morals, without values, is not education—it is foolishness and self-deception. We have no signposts, no road signs, and we have lost direction. Let us look more closely at the connection between principles and moral order.

PRINCIPLES, MORALITY, AND AMERICAN SOCIETY

Morality describes the good and beneficial behavior of individuals and society in response to true principles. Immorality describes behavior apart from principle. Immorality results from the loss of principle in the fabric of the life of an indi-

76

vidual, a culture, or a nation. Without guiding principles that are respected, adhered to, and enforced by a society and its members, everyone gradually drifts to doing that which is "right" in his own eyes. Chaos is the inevitable result.

The famous writer, philosopher, and theologian of our last generation, C. S. Lewis, spoke clearly of the role of moral principles in a society. He observed:

> In reality, moral rules are directions for running the human machine. Every moral rule is there to prevent a breakdown, or a strain, or a friction, in running that machine. That is why these rules at first seem to be constantly interfering with our natural inclinations.[3]

We cannot void moral principles or moral laws—we only can ignore them. If we ignore them, we reap the natural and practical consequences of our ignorance or rebellion in very tangible ways—in our finances, our bodies, our families, our society, and our nation. Similarly, the mere fact that I do not either know of, recognize, or choose to respect the law of gravity does not mean I can jump from a plane at 30,000 feet and fly alongside it. If I have failed to educate myself about the law of gravity or have conceived of some concept that denies its existence, I will soon receive a certain education that comes with exceedingly high-priced tuition.

America is paying the "tuition" for an "education" in the consequences of defying principle and moral law. Perhaps you and your family are as well.

Theories change, but genuine principles and moral laws do not. As Lord Acton declared, "Opinions alter, manner changes, creeds rise and fall, but the moral law is written on the tables of eternity."

Another writer, Alexis Carrel, cogently described the interrelationship of moral principle and the culture in these words:

> Moral sense is more important than intelligence. When it disappears from a nation, the whole social structure slowly commences to crumble away. Christianity is not something that we need to lug along and carry. It should carry us, putting a lift and a buoyant spontaneity into life.[4]

VALUES AND PRINCIPLES TO SUSTAIN A NATION

According to Roy Disney, "It's not hard to make decisions when you know what your values are."[5]

Our problem in America as we approach the year 2000 is that we have forfeited values and principles so carefully observed by our Founding Fathers. We then cry that we have no leadership or vision and bemoan the fact that no one seems to be able to make quality decisions.

Bear with me as we take another brief look at the viewpoint of our Founders.

George Washington, in his farewell address as our first president, reminded us:

Reason and experience both forbid us to expect that National morality can prevail in exclusion of religious principle.[6]

John Adams, our second president, brought home this same truth:

Our Constitution was made only for a moral and religious people. It is wholly inadequate to the government of any other.[7]

We have no government armed with power capable of contending with human passions unbridled by morality and religion.[8]

THE SOURCE OF MORAL PRINCIPLE

The oldest dictionary in America was written by the true father of American education, Noah Webster. Webster made it altogether clear as to where the Founding Fathers looked for the moral principle worthy to serve as the building blocks of a society and nation. His words continue to speak:

The moral principles and precepts contained in the Scriptures ought to form the basis of all our civil constitutions and laws. All the miseries and evils which men suffer from vice, crime, ambition, injustice, oppression, slavery, and war, proceed from their despising or neglecting the precepts contained in the Bible.[9]

HOW YOU CAN BECOME AN EXAMPLE OF PRINCIPLED LIVING

It has been said, "If you don't stand for something, you'll fall for anything."[10]

Thomas Jefferson put it like this: "In matters of style, swim with the current; in matters of principle, stand like a rock."[11]

So let me ask you: Are you a man or woman of principle? Are your principles rooted in vacillating feelings of today, tomorrow, or yesterday, or are they the ageless, timeless, and unchangeable principles of your Creator?

Each of us must make a choice. Our choices are not without consequences. America awaits your courageous choice. Your children and grandchildren are waiting, too. Here are steps you can take.

First: Make decisions and govern your behavior based upon the timeless and proven principles given by God, your Creator, in the Bible. If you do not know them, search them out.

Second: Make decisions for behavior that lead to virtue.

Third: Make decisions for behavior leading to truth and integrity.

Fourth: Make decisions for behavior that you would value highly if they were made by your neighbor.

Fifth: Make decisions for behavior that you would like your children and grandchildren to emulate.

Sixth: Make decisions for behavior which will lay the foundation for America's future. Vote your principles—not your pocketbook.

The following word picture painted by Adam Woslever will help us as a nation and as men and women in this desperate hour, as our ship of state lists precariously from moral decay and is buffeted by the stormy winds of unprincipled living and its consequences.

Let us cling to our principles as the mariner clings to his last plank when night and tempest close about him.[12]

*If I would hear the truth,
I must tell the truth.*

CHAPTER SEVEN

Nothing but the Truth

TRUTH HAS BEEN AN ESSENTIAL ingredient of the American character. Just as we have admired those who dared to venture out into unchartered waters and wildernesses in our early life as a nation, so we have admired those who have dared to tell the truth.

OF TRUTH AND CHERRY TREES

Most of us, in our early schooling, were clearly taught to see the link between our personal and national character for truthfulness through the simple boyhood story of George Washington and the cherry tree. As the story goes, George, as an adventurous and active young boy, cut down a cherry tree on the family compound. When his father inquired as to how the cherry tree disappeared, young George summoned his courage and announced, "I cannot tell a lie." He then proceeded to admit to chopping down the tree. Whether the story is truth or folklore I cannot say. But it conveys a simple, yet unmistakable message to our youth and to ourselves:

- Truth is valued;
- Truth is important to pass on to our children;
- Truth in our leadership is an important part of our American heritage.

We can safely say that whether or not the cherry tree account is genuine, the principle of *truth* was a pillar in the life of our first president. Among his own maxims are these choice words:

I hope I shall always possess firmness and virtue enough to maintain what I consider the most enviable of all titles, the character of an "Honest Man."[1]

MIRRORED IMAGES

A mirror is a very important tool which we normally use privately to assist us in determining how others see us publicly. Most people place great value on how they appear to others. We place mirrors in strategic locations so that we can test at appropriate moments the view we present to those with whom we come in contact. Most of us want to present, at least outwardly, a view and image we desire others to believe about us. But how can we inspect the reflection of our inner man and character on those around us? What looking glass reveals our national character?

OUR "LOOKING GLASS" SELF

If we had a choice, most of us would love to have a three-sided mirror arrangement to allow us to see ourselves more completely from different angles and viewpoints.

The secular "looking glass" of our society and nation is a three-sided mirror consisting of polls, politics, and publications. Let's glance for a few moments into each of these three mirrors to gain perspective into our national character for truth.

Publications

The front page of the October 5, 1992 issue of *Time* carries the headline, "LYING—Everybody's Doin' It—(Honest)." The lead article and cover story is entitled, "Lies, Lies, Lies." The subtitle asks the question, "Is anyone around here telling the truth?" The article then goes on to explore our perversion of truth in politics and in our personal lives, concluding that, "Lies flourish...when people no longer understand, or agree on, the rules governing their behavior toward one another."[2]

Politics

The front page of the July 13, 1992, *Newsweek* is headlined, "SEA OF LIES." The lead article chronicles how leadership in

American armed forces covered up and deceived the American people in the matter of an American warship mistakenly shooting down an Iranian airline.[3] But then *Time* tells us in its October 5, 1992, issue, "The public may now assume lying on the part of its representatives because it expects them to lie."[4]

Why does the American public *expect* its representatives to lie? Because representatives are just that—they represent, mirror, or are representative of the people. According to a *Time*/CNN poll conducted in the early fall of 1992, seventy-five percent of Americans believe there is less honesty in government than there was a decade ago.[5] That is quite a statement since less than two decades ago we experienced what we believed to be a low in political ethics in the great coverup of Watergate, and the narrow avoidance of impeachment by then-President Nixon through voluntary resignation.

A study of the Statistical Abstracts of the United States for the period 1973 through 1985 shows a dramatic increase in federal prosecutions for corruption of public officials—484 percent. If our representatives are indeed representative of American society, we stand indicted as a society. It's easy to say, "Down with the politicians," or "Kick out the bums." But what will we get as replacements from the general cut of "we the people"? For that answer, we might turn to the polls.

Polls

In 1991, Patterson and Kim, advertising executives with the J. Walter Thompson Company, published a moral portrait of the American people entitled, *The Day America Told the Truth*. Their results quantify our personal ethics, values, and beliefs as a people, based upon the largest survey of private morals ever undertaken in any country on earth. Their goal? To probe beneath the public position of Americans to see what we really believe. Chapter four of their book is entitled, "American Liars." These are strong words. They are offensive to our sensibility about whom we want others to think we are, or wish we were. But Patterson and Kim's exhaustive research reveals that ninety-one percent of us lie regularly—"conscious, premeditated lies."[6] They conclude, "Lying has become a cultural trait in America. Lying is embedded in our national character."[7]

We are in national disgrace. What a demoralizing tribute to

the lofty vision of our first president, George Washington, who had declared the most enviable of all titles to be "the character of an Honest Man."

How could a nation known throughout the world for its virtue up until the mid-1900s have turned so rapidly? One key may be found in the results of another poll done in 1990 by George Barna and summarized in his book, *What Americans Believe*. Barna reports, "Most disheartening of all...is the discovery that two-thirds of adults agree that there is no such thing as absolute truth."[8] Even more shocking was his finding that "adults associated with mainline Protestant churches are more likely than all other adults to agree that there is no such thing as absolute truth (seventy-five percent)."[9]

This is truly unnerving. As researcher Barna reports, "More than ever before we are witnessing the entrenchment of what some refer to as 'secular humanist' attitudes."[10] And it appears to be coming from many of the pulpits of America—from those who have been entrusted to tell us the truth. Some others may refer to such thinking as relativistic. The life effect of such thinking is that "people are responsible only to themselves."[11] Patterson and Kim observed, "We no longer can tell right from wrong."[12]

SOCIAL CONSEQUENCES

What might we expect to see from a "breakdown of truth" in our lives? I suggest it is exactly what we are now experiencing:

Distrust of all of our institutions...
- of government;
- of law enforcement;
- of religious leaders;
- of business;
- of marriage.

Loss of leadership;

Fear, doubt, uncertainty, anxiety, and depression;

Crime;

Confusion;

Alienation of men from each other; and

Alienation from God and His blessing on our land.

WHAT IS TRUTH?

Truth has become of such little value in current society that it now is the subject of much humor. By way of illustration, not long ago I was preparing to speak to a particular group. Knowing I am a lawyer, the master of ceremonies set forth the following scenario as part of his introduction. He said:

A man gathered his three trusted counselors about him—his psychologist, his accountant, and his lawyer—to pose to them a most profound question: "What is 1 + 1?" To which question the psychologist replied, "What do you feel it should be?" The accountant queried, "What do you need it to be?" And the lawyer, in "true" allegiance to his client, responded, "What can we make it to be?"

This, unfortunately, is the current perception of truth among our fellow Americans today. But the wanderings of our thinking have not changed much over the last two thousand years. A Roman governor named Pontius Pilate stood as judge of the land over Jesus Christ, who had been brought before him by those leaders of his day who valued power more than purity. The words of that governor will continue to ring out throughout history, "What is truth?"[13]

As Americans, if we have any hope of restoring faith in our government, our marriages, our businesses, and ourselves, we must answer this question—and answer it honestly. Truth must become what it is and ought to be and not what I want it to be.

TO TELL OR NOT TO TELL THE TRUTH, THAT IS THE QUESTION

To tell the truth I must know the truth. In matters of fact or principle, there is only one truth. Truth as to facts or principles has nothing to do with my feelings, my goals, my needs, or my wants. It is what it is—*truth*.

Thomas Jefferson, our third president and drafter of the Declaration of Independence, reflected, "Honesty is the first chapter in the book of wisdom."[14] According to Shakespeare, "No legacy is so rich as honesty."[15] To tell the truth, I must tell the *truth*.

There is a standard for truth. Without a standard, there is no truth. Truth becomes whatever I want it to be, whatever suits my purposes at a given moment. Truth only can be measured or evaluated as against an objective standard. Our Founding Fathers held high the standard for truth—the Bible—as the expression of an all-knowing and loving Creator to his creation. It was their final authority. It was the foundation for freedom. Upon that standard, they founded this nation of freedom. Benjamin Franklin declared, "He who shall introduce into public affairs the principles of primitive Christianity will change the face of the world."[16]

Truth and freedom are inseparable. Our nation's founders embraced the words of Jesus Christ, "If you continue in my word...you will know the truth, and the truth will make you free."[17] Have you embraced the truth of your Creator? What truth do you embrace? Is it dependable? Can you build a life upon it? Can you rebuild a nation upon it? Do you even care?

A COMMITMENT FOR AMERICANS WHO CARE

With every witness I call to the stand to testify at trial, the court reporter stands and asks the witness to stand and repeat after him or her the following words (which I have changed from "oath" to "promise" to meet the objections of those who do not believe it is appropriate to take an "oath"). Will you now stand before God, your children and grandchildren, your spouse, your business associates, the IRS, and your fellow Americans and repeat after me?

I do now solemnly promise to tell the *truth*, the *whole* truth, and *nothing but the truth*, so help me God.

The future of your children depends upon your commitment to truth. Your grandchildren will reap the blessing of your honesty...or the curse of your prevarication. A nation is looking to you—and to me. If you are telling the truth and living the truth in the little things, you will make a major impact in the big things. America's future is in your mouth, and in your heart.

If I am not willing to honestly report my income and expenses at tax time, how can I expect my senator to report his? If I am not willing to return monies to a store clerk who gave me too much change, how can I expect a businessman not to "rip me off"? If I am not willing to be true to my wife, how can I expect her to be true to me? If I tell my employer I'm sick and then go play golf, how can I expect my child not to cut school?

Do you care for your country? Do you care enough to tell and live the truth, the whole truth, and nothing but the truth? Your example of *truthfulness* is the key to restoring the glory, prosperity, and blessing of our nation. May God, through truth lived out in your life, bless America, and may His truth march on in your boots and mine.

If I would have virtue,
I must be virtuous;
If I would have morality,
I must be moral;
If I would have goodness,
I must be good.

CHAPTER EIGHT

The Lamp of Virtue

A MAN, AS THE STORY is told, approached a woman and inquired whether she would sleep with a man other than her husband for a million dollars. After a brief hesitation, she stated that she would. The man then asked, "Would you do it for five dollars?" She replied, "No, what kind of woman do you think I am?" The man responded, "I already found out what kind of woman you are. I merely wanted to find your price."

It is said that ninety-five percent of humor is tragedy in retrospect. Whether this story be actually true or a mere illustration, it conveys with an element of humor the tragedy of the current moral decadence in American society today.

VIRTUE AND THE AMERICAN IMAGE

When was the last time you heard someone use the word *virtue*? Have you ever used the word? Certainly the word *virtue* has lost its place in American parlance. It has become disfavored as a word because virtue has become disfavored as something to be desired or preserved. It is no longer "politically correct." But where have we gone?

America was once known as the land of virtue. Our national symbols frequently included the word *virtue*. Virtue was an essential ingredient to the American way of life. It was the element that bound us together. In 1830, Daniel Webster stated, "Union we reached only by the discipline of our virtues in the severe school of adversity."[1] Virtue was a necessary part of true liberty and independence. For that reason it was spoken in concert with liberty and independence in banners depicting all that was America.

WHAT IS VIRTUE?

Virtue is not a plague. Virtue is moral goodness. It is purity in heart, in motivation, in intention. It is morally sound behavior. Virtuous behavior is that which seeks the best for those around us. It is not self-serving but other serving.

The Statue of Liberty, which most of us still hold dear as a symbol of our nation, is a symbol of virtue—of moral goodness. It was envisioned by its sculptor as a beacon of America's liberty and virtue to the world. The world felt and experienced an unusual "goodness" emanating from the American experiment. This goodness was the fruit of the tree whose roots went deep into the soil of righteousness and right living, which our early founders sought to plant on these shores.

A LIGHT OR ENLIGHTENMENT

The Statue of Liberty was envisioned and sculpted by a Frenchman, Frederic Bartholdi. His vision for this memorial to liberty was sown at about the time our Civil War was concluding. Six decades had passed since France had experienced its revolution near the time of the American Revolution. The French Revolution was a product of the "Age of Enlightenment." The "enlightenment" had severed man's freedom from its roots of religious faith and morality—turning liberty into license. The result in France was moral and political chaos. There was yearning for a republican form of government and a constitution.

America, on the other hand, had experienced a tremendous surge of virtue, righteousness, and goodness that permeated every aspect of American culture. Another Frenchman, Alexis de Tocqueville, upon studying the "American experiment" just twenty-five years before the dream of the Statue of Liberty was born, concluded: "Not until I went into the churches of America and heard her pulpits flame with righteousness did I understand the secret of her genius and power."[2]

America was blazing a "light" across the seas at the very time the Age of Enlightenment was resulting in moral decay and darkness in Europe.

A BEACON OF VIRTUE

The Statue of Liberty was dedicated October 28, 1886. The seven spikes in Liberty's crown represent the seven continents of the world and the seven seas. Inscribed on the tablet held in her hand is the date of our Declaration of Independence.

Bartholdi first conceived the statue would be a lighthouse—shedding a beacon light across the sea from its crown. He entitled it "Liberty Enlightening the World." In 1877, Congress accepted the statue as a "beacon," authorizing it to be administered by the Light-House Board. Later, the torch was resculpted and became a beacon as well, radiating the light of liberty and virtue as far as the eye could see.

A SYMBOL OF MORAL CHARACTER

By World War I, the Statue of Liberty had grown in the heart and soul of America to symbolize the moral character of

America. After the flag, it became "our" symbol.

But the famous, beloved words of poet Emma Lazarius, inscribed in bronze inside the statue, have become tarnished and have an uncertain ring:

Give me your tired, your poor,
Your huddled masses yearning to breathe free,
The wretched refuse of your teeming shore.
Send these, the homeless, tempest-tost to me,
I lift my lamp beside the golden door!

A LAMP GROWN DIM

The beacon light of American liberty and virtue has grown very dim. America is quickly gaining a reputation throughout the world for vice rather than virtue.

The seventy-fifth anniversary edition of America's premier business magazine, *Forbes,* published September 14, 1992, headlines, "A De-moralized Society." The article, with illuminating brilliance, brings focus to the grave nature of our national condition. The following quotes will help us see the issue simply and clearly:

... moral concepts, still more moral judgments, are understood to be somehow undemocratic and unseemly.

We pride ourselves on being liberated from such retrograde Victorian notions.

Today we have so completely rejected the Victorian ethos that we deliberately, systematically, divorce morality from public policy.

In the current climate of moral relativism and skepticism, it is thought improper to impose any moral conditions or requirements....

We are now confronting the consequences of this policy of moral "neutrality."

We are discovering that the economic and social aspects of these problems are inseparable from the moral and psychological ones.

And having made the most determined effort to devise remedies that are "value-free," we find that these policies imperil the material, as well as the moral, well-being of their intended beneficiaries—and not only of individuals but of society as a whole.

... We have demoralized society itself.[3]

WHEN THE LIGHT OF VIRTUE DIMS

It is common knowledge that crime increases as darkness falls. With the dawn of light, misdeeds diminish. So it is that as the beacon light of virtue and morality has been quenched by purposeful and systematic snuffing of the candles of individual and social values, we see crime and numerous other consequences of "darkness" flood in upon us.

If the problem were not so serious, it may seem almost humorous. It is difficult to comprehend how seemingly intelligent, adult Americans can have slipped so far as to, for all practical purposes, call black "white" and white "black." We call immorality "choices," and we call the pursuit of virtue "bigotry," "rightist," "fundamentalist." Folks, our lamp is going out. We are groping our way in the late dusk of American society. In the words of the 1960s musical duo Simon and Garfunkel, "...the words of the prophets are written on the subway walls...." They are "the sounds of silence"[4]—moral silence.

THE SOUNDS OF SILENCE

Let's look into the darkening windows of American society for a glimpse of the consequences of our dismissing virtue as "old fashioned" and embracing moral "neutrality," both individually and as a nation. Perhaps our best insight is found in *The Day America Told the Truth,* a 1991 summary of the massive research and investigation by two advertising executives on what Americans really believe and do.

- Sixty percent of Americans have been victims of crime at least once.
- Fifty-eight percent of Americans have been victimized twice or more.
- There were twenty million crimes against the "persons" of Americans in 1988 alone.
- There are more than 25,000 homicides in America each year now—more than in any other industrialized country.

97

- Only thirty percent of Americans are loyal to their companies.
- Twenty-five percent of Americans will compromise their beliefs to get ahead on the job. But sixty-six percent of high school seniors would lie to achieve an important business objective.
- Ninety-one percent of Americans lie regularly—conscious, premeditated lies.
- 2.2 million Americans believe they have AIDS. Another 7 million believe they are "high risk" for AIDS. But more than one-third would not tell their lovers.
- One out of every seven Americans carries a weapon in their car or on their person—that is twenty-six million people.
- One third of Americans have contemplated suicide.
- The U.S. has twenty times the number of rapes reported in Japan, England, and Spain.
- Children's TV programming averages twenty-five violent acts per hour. That is up fifty percent from the early 1980s.
- Twenty percent of Americans lose their virginity before age thirteen.
- Sixty-one percent of Americans now eighteen to twenty-four years of age lost their virginity by age sixteen.
- Thirty-one percent of all married Americans have had an affair. Sixty-two percent think there is nothing morally wrong with their affairs.
- Over fifty percent of Americans accept "living together" as an acceptable alternative to marriage.
- Ninety-two percent of sexually active Americans have had ten or more lovers.[5]

Friends, if these facts do not cause your American gut to wrench and your mind and heart to grasp out for pillars of personal and national morality and virtue to keep balance, we are without hope. As described by the secular writers of *The Day America Told the Truth*, "For a fistful of dollars, we found that Americans would do almost anything: lie, cheat, steal, murder, abandon their families, and change their religion."[6] The writers conclude:

> It's been said that an era comes to an end when its dreams are exhausted. America's dreams are wearing extremely thin—at least the kind of dreams that can sustain a great nation.[7]

VIRTUE IS NOT A FOUR-LETTER WORD

We have been led to believe by the most vocal elements of our society these last forty years that virtue is "out" and moral neutrality is "in." Many have been branded with labels for speaking up for that which was right and honorable. Labels and characterizations mold us and make us feel that somehow we are not in the mainstream of society. Since mankind's greatest needs are to be loved and to be accepted, we have defaulted on virtue and standing for morality to avoid feeling rejected. We have been made to feel as if "virtue" is a four-letter word.

I have good news for you! To quote *Forbes* business magazine, September 14, 1992, "Liberal intellectuals have, in short, divorced themselves not only from conventional morality but also from those conventional people who still adhere to that morality."[8] "After decades of silence and denial, it is now finally respectable to speak of the need for 'traditional values'—moral values, family values, social values."[9] The author of the article added, "[We must] encourage a 'counter-counterculture' that will resist the now entrenched 'counterculture.'"[10]

LET US REBUILD AMERICAN VIRTUE

Here is wisdom. The French Nobel Prize winner, Alexis Carrel, who spent many years in America, stated, "Virtue roots us firmly in reality. A virtuous individual is like an engine in good working order. It is due to lack of virtue that the weaknesses and disorders of modern society are due."[11]

George Washington, in his farewell address, like a prophet warned the fledgling nation that:

> Of all the dispositions and habits which lead to political prosperity, religion and morality are indispensable supports. Let us with caution indulge the supposition that morality can be maintained without religion.... Reason and experience both forbid us to expect that National

morality can prevail in exclusion of religious principle.[12]

Forty years later, Alexis de Tocqueville, when he came from France to observe the prosperity of America, noted, "...the religious aspect of the country was the first thing that struck my attention."[13] "I do not know whether all Americans have a sincere faith in their religion—for who can search the human heart? But I am certain they hold it to be indispensable to the maintenance of republican institutions."[14] "...It belongs to the whole nation and to every rank of society."[15] "Christian morality is everywhere the same."[16]

He went on to reflect on his 1840 observations:

In the United States the sovereign authority is religious, and consequently hypocrisy must be common; but there is no country in the world where the Christian religion retains a greater influence over the souls of men than in America; and there can be no greater proof of its utility...than that its influence is powerfully felt over the most enlightened and free nation on earth.[17]

Virtue and morality require a base, a foundation. Genuine virtue and true morality do not change. They are rooted in the laws of God.

Noah Webster, founder of American education, wrote: "The moral principles and precepts contained in the Scriptures ought to form the basis of all our civil constitutions and laws. All the miseries which men suffer from vice, crime, ambition, injustice, oppression, slavery, and war proceed from their despising, neglecting the precepts contained in the Bible."[18]

VIRTUE BEGINS AT HOME

The April 27, 1992 issue of *Time* magazine included an essay by Charles Krauthammer entitled, "In Praise of Mass Hypocrisy." In the essay, he stated, "...as voters we profess shock that our candidates should behave as we do.... The paradox is striking: voters are demanding in their leaders the personal virtues that they decreasingly demand of themselves." He then declares, "There is a word for the profession of virtue accompanied by the practice of vice: hypocrisy."[19]

Virtue begins at home. It begins with the little things. It begins with not calling in "sick" at work when I want to go shopping. It means not having my secretary say, "He's not in," when I don't want to talk to someone. Give God a crack into your mind, your thoughts, your inner being—your heart. What does He see? What do you see there?

If you were to sell your character, would you get full retail, or would it go for a bargain-basement price?

Alexis de Tocqueville warned us, "America is great because America is good, and if America ever ceases to be good, America will cease to be great."

If America's future depends on your example of virtue and morality, what is America's future?

If I would have honor,
I must be honorable.

CHAPTER NINE

Our Sacred Honor

THE GLORY OF AMERICAN LIBERTY was born in the light of American honor.

July 4 is a day of national celebration for all Americans. On that day, one of mankind's greatest declarations was signed, declaring the birth of a nation that would change the world and make it a better place. As we revel in fireworks and hang out the Stars And Stripes each year, few are conscious of the high cost that purchased the liberty we enjoy.

On July 4, 1776, fifty-six courageous men gathered in Philadelphia to fix their names to the Declaration of Independence. Most of them were Englishmen at heart. They anguished over the manner in which the mother country had so tyrannized the thirteen colonies. King George and the English Parliament seemed bent on making second-class citizens of the colonists and repressing them with taxation without representation. Basic God-given rights were being ignored, and the people were exploited.

Tensions were high...explosive! Although most of the signers had been fundamentally loyal to the Crown, they were now convinced "the laws of Nature and of Nature's God" required that they individually and collectively take a stand for human dignity and against tyranny.

They found "these truths to be self-evident, that all men are created equal, that they are endowed by their Creator with certain inalienable rights...." To this end, they declared their independence from an earthly power, England, and declared their dependence upon a heavenly power—God Himself.

The fifty-six signers of the Declaration of Independence were the business, professional, scientific, political, and spiritual leaders of their day. Many of them were wealthy. Most of the rest were men of means. They had families. Many had position and fame. They were prominent and prosperous. And they realized their declaration of principle could turn their prosperity to poverty. They also considered the grave reality that if they lost in their bid for freedom, they would feel a traitor's rope tighten on their necks.

In this crucible of human drama, fifty-six men decided liberty was more important than life—that principle was more important than prosperity. And they fixed their names boldly to the Declaration. We must carefully and prayerfully now reconsider the closing words of that Declaration:

> With a firm reliance on the protection of Divine Providence, we mutually pledge to each other our lives, our fortunes, and our sacred honor.

THE PRICE OF HONOR

Calvin Coolidge, a former president of the United States, made a piercing observation that each of us might well consider. He said, "No person was ever honored for what he received. Honor has been the reward for what he gave."[1]

What did our Founding Fathers give in pledging their sacred honor? Of the fifty-six:

- Five were captured by the British and tortured before they died;
- Twelve had their homes sacked, occupied by the British, or burned;
- Two lost their sons in the army;
- One had two sons captured;
- Nine died in the war, either from bullets or from the stresses.[2]

They considered their honor "sacred." That which is sacred is precious, worthy of preservation, worthy of protection. It is worth living for and, therefore, worth dying for.

On the day the Declaration of Independence was signed, John Adams declared to his wife, Abigail:

> I am well aware of the toil, and blood, and treasure that it will cost to maintain this declaration, and support and defend these states; yet, through all the gloom I can see the rays of light and glory. I can see that the end is worth all the means.[3]

His son, John Quincy Adams, also a president of our nation, reflected:

> Posterity—you will never know how much it has cost my generation to preserve your freedom. I hope you will make good use of it.[4]

SHALL THESE DEAD HAVE DIED IN VAIN?

Undoubtedly one of the most vocal spokesmen of the American Revolution was Patrick Henry. The drama of his "Give me liberty or give me death" plea is unforgettable to us even today—at least in our minds. But in our hearts I fear we little understand its significance. It expressed a willingness to give all—yes, even my sacred honor—for the cause of God-given liberty.

Thomas Payne also was a vital spokesman during the American Revolution. Let's consider his statement:

> What we obtain too cheaply, we esteem too lightly; it is dearness only that gives everything its value. Heaven knows how to put a price upon its goods, and it would be strange indeed if so celestial an article as freedom should not be highly rated.[5]

Thomas Jefferson expressed his concern similarly, crying out from his inward being, from his sacred honor:

> My God! how little do my countrymen know what precious blessings they are in possession of, and which no other people on earth enjoy.[6]

What do we make of such service, such sacrifice, such honor today? Do we revere it? Do we respect its fruits? Do we honor the blood of these men? Their lives? Their vision? Or has our freedom, our nation under God, taken short shrift in the face of our headlong pursuit of personal freedom and affluence? Jefferson minced no words when he declared, "The price of liberty is eternal vigilance."[7] Are we paying the price? Or is liberty and honor no longer valued? Were the efforts of these men ultimately in vain?

AMERICA'S HALL OF FAME/SHAME

Honor springs from the well of moral living. Without moral virtue, the glory of honor recedes behind the glare of vice. The first king of Israel discovered this truth when he rendered only partial obedience to God's command to him. God had exalted Saul from obscurity to kingship. In his kingly pride, Saul decided he would "do his own thing," believing that as long as he gave lip service and partial compliance to God's expectations, God would see things his way. God was not impressed. He sent the prophet Samuel to King Saul with a biting message:

To obey is better than sacrifice, and to hearken than the fat of rams.[8]

King Saul lost the moral light that raised him to honor, and his glory faded to disgrace.

America stands in a similar position today. The God who gave us life gave us liberty. He inspired our Founding Fathers, instilling in them the moral and spiritual light that revealed the path and blazed the way for development of the government and social fabric of a nation, the light of which has radiated to the entire world. That light produced a glory rooted in national virtue and honor. But as we have become proud and self-sufficient, we thought we could ignore that Divine Friend and His plans for life and prosperous living. We agreed with the popular song saying, "I'll do it my way." And we have. But not without consequence. Our honor is tarnished, and our glory is turning to shame.

Chapter 6 of Patterson and Kim's *The Day America Told the Truth* is entitled, "The American Hall of Shame." In that chapter, the two advertising executives inspect the behavior of Americans as reflected from the minds and hearts of Americans as we view ourselves. Their conclusion: America is in shame.[9]

What is especially frightening, though, is that we are even losing our sense of shame. We have seared our moral conscience. Chapter 12 of *The Day America Told the Truth* bears the title, "Infidelity: It's Rampant."[10] We are then told, "Almost one-third of all married Americans have had or are now having an affair."[11] "Today, the majority of Americans (sixty-two percent) think that there is nothing morally wrong with the affairs they're having."[12]

So much for honor. Whatever happened to the Marine Corps motto, *"SEMPER FIDELIS"*—always faithful? If I cannot be faithful to my spouse, how can I be faithful to my country? If I cannot be faithful to these, to what am I faithful? Where is my honor? I cannot even be faithful to myself. Hence, the increasing wave of suicides and flocking to "shrinks" and "tea leaf" readers. Yet we sport license plates declaring our "independence": "SCREW GUILT." Folks, we are losing our liberty because we are losing our honor.

FLICKERING EMBERS

As a public speaker and author, I have gathered resource books around me as tools of the trade. Of particular interest to me have been books compiling thousands of quotations, broken down into various subject categories. This enables me to very quickly probe the halls of history for the thoughts of sages past, as well as more current thinking. I have used four such reference books for many years but recently acquired several more, which promised to be helpful. I opened my older volumes to the key word *honor* and quickly found a number of quotations in each. But when I searched the three new acquisitions, I was grieved that the word *honor* did not even appear. Each one of these new volumes seemed to have many more quotations than any of the old standbys, yet no "honor." What was especially shocking is that one of the books purports to be a large collection of "American" quotations and the other two of "religious" quotations—yet no "honor."

Not only are we losing our honor in fact...we are even being stripped of the memory of honor. We must put new kindling on the flickering embers of honor. It is a cold and selfish world, nation, family, and heart without honor. It is the ultimate demise of a civilized people—yes, even of the nation itself.

SO MUCH FOR HEROES

One of the saddest consequences of the demise of honor is the disappearance of heroes. America has been rich in heroes— men and women who stood for truth, who courageously did and spoke what was right. Names like George Washington, John Adams, Abraham Lincoln, Paul Revere, Florence Nightingale, John Paul Jones, Davy Crocket, Daniel Boone, Charles Finney, Winthrop, Bradford, Dwight Moody, Billy Sunday, and Billy Graham dot the American memory. Their memory enriches our spirit and lifts us to higher ground.

But where have all the heroes gone? We shifted from statesmen and courageous moral leaders to athletes and superstars of the entertainment world, most of whom have epitomized anything but sound moral fiber with which to feed our youth.[13] Even Superman is now dead.

According to a recent poll, seventy percent of Americans believe there are no living heroes today. About the same number say that our children have no meaningful role models. Neither do we trust our leaders or institutions—not even ourselves.[14] As the ballad from the decade of the sixties croons, "When will we ever learn?" No power from without could do to us what we have done to ourselves.

AN AWAKENING CONSCIENCE

Historian Paul Johnson, writing for the seventy-fifth anniversary edition of *Forbes* magazine, observes that we have embraced a "secularized utopianism" in the twentieth century, believing "that society can be made comfortable, safe, healthy, and secure for all, irrespective of merit or effort, and that the agency of this process is the state." He concludes that this "secular utopia" has not and cannot be realized and that its pursuit has been at enormous cost to an entire generation. Americans, he feels, still have a "strong, deep-rooted moral sense" and see the current severe troubling throughout our society as evidence of a "returning sense of wrongdoing"—an "awakened conscience."[15] Perhaps these are indeed the flickering embers. If so, where do we go from here?

IS THERE HONOR AMONG THIEVES?

It has been said there is honor among thieves. Such "honor," however, when limited to a macro society of general lawlessness

110

does little to benefit society as a whole. Yet in current American society we have multitudes of little bands of "thieves," little groups, clubs, families, businesses, even churches where we honor one another within the ranks for our various deeds of "service," but where our behavior and heart toward the citizens and society outside is often less than honorable. It is not that we *intend* to be dishonorable, we just are...because the disease has so pervasively infected us as a people.

So we cannot "bootstrap" honor. Honor comes from within. It issues from the inner character—from the heart. And honor is then bestowed by society back to one who has acted honorably from his heart. So what is the means whereby we can restore honor to our hearts and lives individually and as a nation? The answer is not "blowing in the wind." It is simple and straight-forward.

RESTORING THE ROOTS OF HONOR

Our Founding Fathers were nearly universal in their conviction as to the root of honor. They were convinced, as declared by George Washington himself, that, "Of all the dispositions and habits which lead to political prosperity, Religion and morality are indispensable supports."[16]

They were also convinced that "national morality cannot prevail in exclusion of religious principle."[17]

But it was not religion in general that moved them. It was the Christian faith as expressed in the Bible—the Holy Scriptures. Noah Webster could not state this fundamental belief more clearly:

> The moral principles and precepts contained in the Scriptures ought to form the basis of all our civil constitutions and laws. All the miseries and evils which men suffer from vice, crime, ambition, injustice, oppression, slavery, and war, proceed from their despising or neglecting the precepts contained in the Bible.[18]

This understanding of the Bible as the root of American morality, honor, and success carried forward 150 years as reflected by our presidents.

> All the good from the Savior of the world is communicated through this Book; but for the Book we could not

know right from wrong. All the things desirable to man are contained in it.[19]

—Abraham Lincoln

The foundations of our society and our government rest so much on the teachings of the Bible that it would be difficult to support them if faith in these teachings would cease to be practically universal in our country.[20]

—Calvin Coolidge

DESPISING OR NEGLECTING

As we have seen, Noah Webster made it clear that all of the evils and miser*ies of men proceed from either DESPISING or NEGLECTING* the precepts contained in the Bible. While there are some scorners who apparently despise the Bible as the Word of God, most Americans would fortunately not yet be so pridefully arrogant.

But that does not leave us with excuse. Most of us are guilty of what we believe to be "benign" neglect. We do not intend to neglect. We just don't specifically intend not to. We do not intend harm. We just blithely disregard potential conse-quences...or figure, "What I don't know won't hurt me." Some of us pride ourselves, just as did Israel's first king, on our belief in the Bible, on how often we go to church, on what good things we are doing for God. But we selectively leave out those things He requires of us that are inconvenient or inconsistent with our current agenda.

According to the Author's view of His Holy Word, no neglect is "benign." He expects us to take heed, to listen, and to act accordingly. Honor will follow.

One of the most noble, honorable and classic films of our time was *Chariots of Fire.* In a moment of moral choice and crisis, Eric Liddell, the young Olympian upon whose life the film was based, made a personal decision choosing God's way rather than yield to the pressure of political power in his nation. He was a man of principle and honor. He was willing to sacri-fice temporary personal pleasure and goals in favor of God's eternal plan and principles. And he was honored by both God and man. In his moment of decision, he sought direction from the Bible and relied upon God's promise:

> "...them that honor Me
> I will honor..."[21]

If we would see the light and the glory of America return, we must restore her honor. Woodrow Wilson's words advise us well:

> "The nation's honor is dearer than the nation's comfort;
> Yes, than the nation's life itself."[22]

But there is no national honor without individual honor.

THE HONOR OF HUMILITY

Humility is the soil condition of the heart and character out of which honor grows and is manifested. The Scriptures advise:

> "...Before honor is humility."[23]

But the same passage warns, "Before destruction the heart of man is haughty."[24] God hates pride. So do most people. But God honors humility in a man, woman, and nation. He has promised, "Humble yourselves therefore under the mighty hand of God, that he may exalt you in due time."[25] But He warns, "...the nation and kingdom that will not serve thee shall perish."[26]

Humble service to God and our fellow man is the hallmark of honor.

HONOR OF SACRIFICE

It was said by George Sand, "There is but one virtue—the eternal sacrifice of self."[27] O. P. Clifford similarly stated, "The altar of sacrifice is the touchstone of character."[28]

I would like to close this chapter by sharing with you thoughts from one of America's most honored and successful businessmen and entrepreneurs—J. C. Penny, founder of the J. C. Penny chain of stores. The founding motto of the J. C. Penny Company was, "Honor, Confidence, Service, and Cooperation."[29] Mr. Penny encourages and guides us with these words in his autobiography, *Fifty Years With the Golden Rule:*

As to our country, my faith in our America, in its people and in the "American way of life" is unwavering. Its founding I believe to have been divinely ordained, and God has a mighty mission for it among the nations of the world. It was founded in prayer, in faith, and in the heroic spirit of sacrifice. Lives of comparative ease might have been the lot of our forefathers in their own country had they been willing to surrender their convictions. They chose the "hard right," rather than the "easy wrong"....[30]

As a nation, and as individuals, our fate will always be determined by our choice of the "hard right" or the "easy wrong"...[31]

Every aspect of world condition today opens a way provocatively for applying Christian principles to living. Let us not be afraid: loving God, and our neighbors as ourselves, let us only believe. Being not afraid, and believing, let us choose for ourselves the "hard right." If individuals in sufficient number will pledge their part as men willing to follow the hard right, our America will be made safe for her own people and will stand as a beacon light of hope to this war-torn, war-weary world.[32]

My American friend, will you join with me in that pledge? Regardless of the branch of the armed services in which you may have served, will you, in the words of the Marine Corps hymn, be "First to fight for right and freedom, and to keep our *honor* clean"?

I pray that you will, for America is depending on you. From our ancestors came our names; from our virtues, our honor. Leave your children and your grandchildren a heritage of honor. And may God bless you accordingly.

*Fidelity is the heart of trust
and the mind of commitment.*

Chapter Ten

Semper Fi

NOWHERE IS HONOR BETTER EXEMPLIFIED than in fidelity. Fidelity is an essential ingredient to honor. Without fidelity, there is no honor. And yet the very word *fidelity* has largely been lost from our culture, our conversation, and our character as Americans. It is now most frequently found as part of the names of our financial institutions such as Fidelity Federal Savings. But in our lives and conversation, fidelity has largely become a lost art.

How is it I can become concerned with fidelity when it comes to my money but can take it or leave it when it comes to the more important issues of life—people, principles, and purpose? Perhaps when we can answer that question we will also be able to explain how we can dispense with character when electing our politicians, in favor of their economic promises. If character is not an issue during an election, then I have no right to make it an issue after the election.

The life quality of fidelity, or the lack thereof, pervades every fiber of our personal and national character. It is interrelated with both our vices and our virtues. It lies at the root of both our honors and our horrors.

AMERICA'S CLASSIC CONTRAST

America's Hall of Honor

He was a graduate of Yale in the Class of 1773, and taught in a girls' school while preparing for the ministry. When news of the "shot heard 'round the world" from the Battle of Lexington and Concord reached him, he immediately enlisted in the Connecticut Rangers to fight the tyranny of the British. At a town meeting he declared, "Liberty? Independence? Are they to remain only words? Gentlemen, let us make them fighting words!"

General Washington desperately needed intelligence information about British intentions. This delicate assignment was given to the young captain. Disguised as a schoolmaster, he infiltrated British lines, making sketches and taking notes in Latin. He was captured after taking a wrong boat on his way back to the American encampment, and readily admitted his identity.

The following day, September 22, 1776, the twenty-one-year-old captain was executed by hanging, without a trial. There was sobbing among witnesses, but he never lost his composure. As they put the noose around his neck, he declared, "I only regret that I have but one life to lose for my country."[1] The name of Nathan Hale has been immortalized in America's Hall of Honor. He was true to himself, true to his conscience, and true to his country.

America's Hall of Shame

He was given high command in the Continental Army. Despite his courage and brilliance, his ego and flamboyant ways raised eyes of distrust among many. He staged elaborate banquets, rode in gaudy carriages, and caused many to wonder how he could finance such lavish living. He also developed unusually close relationships with British sympathizers. When Congress acted to investigate his business deals, in retaliation he began selling his services to the British.

Due to his military brilliance, General Washington offered him command of the left wing of the American Army, but command of West Point was granted by specific request. The man immediately took steps to turn over West Point—gateway to the entire Hudson region—for a price. He sought full details on all secret agents working for the American command. But no real suspicion of treachery ever entered the mind of General Washington or his other commanders.

On September 23, 1776, the day after Nathan Hale was hung, a British agent was caught by American militiamen. A search revealed documents in the handwriting of the commander of West Point hidden in the agent's shoe, which would have set the stage for the British to divide the colonies. The conspiracy failed and the traitorous American commander of West Point escaped.

He received reward from the British as the price of his prostituted fidelity—6,315 British pounds and an annual pension of 500 pounds for his wife. Offsetting his reward was a future of disgrace. The name of Benedict Arnold is immortalized in America's Hall of Shame. His life was tormented by the hatred of the Americans he had sold out, and corroded by the scorn and distrust of the British who had bought him.[2]

WHAT IS YOUR PRICE?

Are you a Nathan Hale or are you a Benedict Arnold? Can you be bought? Are you true to yourself, to your family, to your conscience, to your countrymen, to your God? Or have you sold out? Have you sold out in little ways? Maybe you did not commit treason against your country; maybe only against your family...or your own conscience.

It has been said, "Conscience is a sacred sanctuary where God alone may enter as judge."[3] Conscience reveals the little things. We know that "...the little foxes, that spoil the vines."[4] The American "vine" is being destroyed by little "foxes." That is true in the area of fidelity as it is in other areas. "Fidelity in small things is at the base of every great achievement," says Charles Wagner.[5]

The ancient Cicero gives us insight into the wisdom of the ages in reflecting:

Nothing is more noble, nothing more venerable than fidelity. Faithfulness and truth are the most sacred excellences and endowments of the human mind.[6]

WHAT IN THE WORLD IS FIDELITY?

We may need to ask ourselves this question: What is fidelity anyway? Certainly we do not use the word in common parlance anymore. But we do hear a familiar ring to its counterpart: *infidelity*. Isn't it interesting that we should be more familiar with "infidelity" than with "fidelity?" Perhaps this is a commentary on where we are as a people and as a nation.

But there are terms that we more commonly use that are relatives of fidelity—words such as *faithfulness, dependability, reliability, commitment, loyalty,* and *duty.* In the pages that follow, we will explore where we are in terms of our individual and national fidelity, and the practical impact of this on our American society and culture. We will inspect the fidelity chain throughout our relationships—fidelity to family, children, spouses, institutions, and our fellow citizens—and how they all relate to our fidelity to God.

FIDELITY TO THE FAMILY

Chapter 7 of George Gallup's book *Forecast 2000*, is entitled "The Faltering Family." Since the family is generally considered to be the building block of our society, perhaps we should begin our exploration there. I quote his first two paragraphs:

> In a recent Sunday school class in a Methodist Church in the Northeast, a group of eight- to ten-year-olds were in a deep discussion with their two teachers. When asked to choose which of ten stated possibilities they most feared happening, their response was unanimous. All the children most dreaded a divorce between their parents.
>
> Later, as the teachers, a man and a woman in their late thirties, reflected on the lesson, they both agreed they'd been shocked at the response. When they were the same age as their students, they said the possibility of their parents being divorced never entered their heads. Yet in just one generation, children seemed to feel much less security in their family ties.[7]

In a poll of opinion leaders, says Gallup, "Thirty-three percent of the responses listed decline of the family structure, divorce, and other family-oriented concerns as one of the five major problems facing the nation today."[8] As a lawyer in the practice of "family" law for the past eighteen years, I am convinced the breakdown of the family is a threat to our national health, strength, security, and integrity, and that this threat is second only to the breakdown of *truth*, which we will look at the conclusion to this chapter.

This is not intended to be an exhaustive study of family life in America. However, its importance is so basic and the consequences of its breakdown so cataclysmic, that we must look a little further. Consider the following:

- Today, one out of every two marriages ends in divorce.
- The rate of divorce has more than doubled in the last two decades.
- About 100,000 people over age fifty-five get divorced in the U.S. each year—usually initiated by men who reach retirement—and break marriages of thirty years' duration or more.
- In 1970, seventy-one percent of all adults were part of a married-couple family. By 1991, only fifty-five percent of adults were in married-couple families.
- Some demographers confidently predict a majority of American adults will be single by the year 2000.[9]

So what is driving the American family into oblivion? What forces are creating these frightening statistics? George Gallup cites four such forces:

- Sexual morality
- Alternative lifestyles
- Economics
- Feminist philosophy[10]

If we take a close look, the conclusion is virtually inescapable that each of these forces or causes of family disintegration finds its root in lack of *fidelity*, or lack of faithfulness. Lack of fidelity is *infidelity*.

Changes in sexual morality are rooted in infidelity. We are no longer committed to sex within the bond of marriage, nor are we committed to be true to our spouses during marriage. Chapter 12 of Patterson and Kim's *The Day America Told the*

Truth is labeled, "Infidelity: It's Rampant..." They state:

- Almost one-third of all married Americans (31%) have had an affair.[11]
- Sixty-two percent of Americans think there is nothing wrong with the affairs they're having.[12]

Marriage infidelity is not our only concern. We are untrue to ourselves before marriage, and untrue to our friends. Chapter 13 of *The Day America Told the Truth* is entitled, "The End of Childhood in America." The authors state:

- Twenty percent of kids lose their virginity before age thirteen.[13]
- Sixty-one percent of eighteen- to twenty-four-year-olds lost their virginity by the age of sixteen.[14]

The January 18, 1993, edition of *Newsweek* carries this front cover headline: "AIDS and the Arts—a Lost Generation."[15] There is no cure for AIDS. Because it is carried predominantly among homosexuals who practice what we are asked to call "an alternative lifestyle," not only is the family itself breached by homosexuality, but the entire family of the human race is threatened; the disease has now spread to heterosexual practitioners through blood or through infidelity.

Infidelity is killing us physically, spiritually, and socially. Infidelity—the failure to be faithful—is at its root *selfishness*. Infidelity goes to the very heart and core of character.

Infidelity often results when women leave the home to work. I want to be sensitive here, but not to the extent the issue is politely avoided. We need to search deeply into our hearts and motivations.

Husband, have you asked your wife to work rather than stay home with the kids because you want another car, a bigger house, or fancier vacations? If so, can you see how your selfish choices could result in infidelity within your family?

Wife and mother, are you motivated to go to work because you "want to be where the action is," want to feel more important, expect to gain your self-worth from the job, or are trying to "improve" your standard of living?

Could it be that the long-range "standard of living" of your family and children might suffer for a choice that was really not truly necessary? Are we sacrificing long-term values for short-term gain? Are we being true? Are we being faithful? Are we telling ourselves the truth? Moms and dads, your family needs *you* more than your money.

In his book, The Future of the American Family, George Barna, pollster and researcher, talks about what he calls *nouveau* families. These *nouveau* or new families are made up of various combinations of persons not related by blood or marriage, even including casual acquaintances—people who care about each other.[16] Young people increasingly define family as "the people who really care about me," rather than parents and siblings.[17] According to Barna, one of the principle causes of this trend toward redefinition of family is that people "believe the traditional family configurations have failed them personally."[18]

Why do an increasing number of people find it necessary to redefine the family? It's due to:
- Child abuse
- Child molestation
- "Latch-key" parenting
- Divorce
- "Child care" instead of parents caring for their children
- Trusting the TV to parent
- Failure to spend personal time with our children
- Failure to spend personal time with our spouses
- All work and no play
- All play and no pray
- Exalting my rights over my responsibilities.

It is family infidelity. It is lack of faithfulness to our calling as parents and spouses. Barna expresses the problem succinctly:

> ... those who advocate such loose family ties often fail to grasp that successful families are successful largely because they offer safety, trust, and permanence. Once a family ceases to offer those protections, the atmosphere for love and intimacy is lost. Ultimately, the family falters because its members refuse to surrender some of their freedoms for the benefit of others.[19]

A SPECIAL WORD TO FATHERS

Dr. James Dobson is widely known as "America's family advocate." As founder and president of the large non-profit organization Focus on the Family, he has spoken widely across America and conducts a daily radio broadcast in response to which he receives many thousands of letters monthly. In his book, *Straight Talk to Men,* Dr. Dobson boldly states:

If America is going to survive the incredible stresses and dangers it now faces, it will be because husbands and fathers again place their families at the highest level on their system of priorities...[20]

The Western world stands at a great crossroads in its history.[21]

...Our very survival as a people will depend on the presence or absence of masculine leadership in millions of homes.[22]

In reference to the numerous letters he receives, Dr. Dobson observes, "One of the most common letters I receive is sent by hundreds of women who ask the same question:

My husband won't assume spiritual leadership in our family. He doesn't seem to be aware of my needs and the requirements of our children. How can I get his attention?[23]

Dr. Dobson strongly contends that "...husbands hold the keys to the preservation of the family."[24] If we hold the keys, what have we done with them? Another writer has said that our real problem is "renegade males."[25] A renegade is one who "reneges." A man who reneges is a man who is not faithful to his calling. He does not provide moral and spiritual leadership in the home. He is more concerned about his work...about Monday-night football...about the news...about anything and everything but what really counts. He has never seriously considered that his children follow his example—that the twig is being bent.

Fathers, we are America's first line of defense. We are also America's primary offense. We must straighten up our act, discipline ourselves to be faithful as "God's hand extended" to our children. We must love them, nurture them, pray with them and for them—and we must love their mother. It has been said,

"The greatest gift a father can give to his children is to love their mother."[26]

Dads, our children are waiting for us. America's future is in our hands. Since America's future *is* in our hands, what will America's future be? Will you be faithful? If you have not been faithful, will you go before your wife and children and ask forgiveness for your failure? Will you then repent, turn, and become the man God created you to be? Fathers are the first hope for America's future. Will you dare to be a father in America?

CHILDREN—FIDELITY WAR CASUALTIES

In my law practice, I have watched in agony as I have seen children pulled and torn in the breakup of homes. No matter how much we rationalize from the depths of our personal pain, children really do need both a mother and a father—yes, in the same house. Barna, in *The Future of the American Family*, quotes a professor of cultural studies, who predicts:

I think we are just beginning to see the results of the devastation we sowed over the last twenty-five years. The deep scars laid on our children as a consequence of our narcissistic, driven way of life cannot be downplayed. For years to come, you will see the ramifications of a divorce-happy, single-parent society when you look at crime statistics, suicide rates, relational crisis, moral ambiguity, and the widespread problems of self-esteem that manifest themselves in a myriad of public and private ways.[27]

Kids do pay a high price! Is it worth it?

We have barely scratched the surface as to the impact of our lack of parental fidelity to our children. Child abuse is now rampant. Having now been brought before the public eye in glaring technicolor, government and the courts have stepped in. As occurs whenever government steps in, there is overreaction. Because we have delegated excessive responsibility to government, government now becomes a significant threat to the family itself, stepping in under color of law to undermine the authority of parents. Social engineers with godless agendas seek to place the state in the role of the "ultimate parent."

Now we even have children divorcing their parents. How

can this be? It is the fruit of the tree of infidelity. The Scriptures warned us that in the last days children would rise up against their parents.[28] We are also admonished that a curse on our society is directly linked to whether or not the hearts of the fathers will be turned to the children, and the hearts of the children to their fathers.[29]

When will we break the cycle? Will you be the first? Will you vow that from this day forward you will be faithful in parenting your children? Will you adjust your priorities—your finances, your time, your energies? Can America depend on you? Can your children?

DUTY IS A FOUR-LETTER WORD

Duty is a word in disrepute. It fell into disfavor as rights became exalted over responsibility in our society. It has largely become "a four-letter word" in the American mind and consciousness. That is consistent with the mortal blows being dealt to fidelity, for "duty" and "fidelity" are close relatives.

It has been said, "Not liberty, but duty, is the condition of existence."[30] The trouble is that so many Americans who are standing up for their rights are falling down on their duties. When duty calls, some people are never at home. Generally speaking, duty is what we have come to expect of *others*. A man never gets so confused in his thinking that he can't see the other fellow's duty.[31]

Our failure, as individuals, to be true and faithful to our fellow citizens has resulted in severe economic crisis and near bankruptcy as a nation. We need some "radical" rethinking of premises we have come to accept as "givens." The following is food for thought:

- If we personally cared for our parents, we may not need Social Security.
- If we personally, or through our churches and clubs, cared for the hungry and homeless in our neighborhood and helped those without jobs find work, we might not need welfare.
- If as an elected official I refused to vote "largess from the public treasury" and fill the "pork barrel" of special

interests, or to exceed funds in a balanced budget, we would not have a federal deficit.

A genuine sense of duty has a way of simplifying matters which loom excessively complex when I want to delegate my duty. These are but a few examples. We have created major problems for ourselves because of our collective refusal as individual Americans to "do our duty." I stand included. We have been, as a people, unfaithful to our national call and purpose. We have mortgaged our future. It is truly "We the people" who must act as individuals—not as a government. We can no longer shirk our responsibilites. Duty calls.

This is not a new issue. In 1802, John Quincy Adams said, when you think of duty, "Think of your forefathers! Think of your posterity!"[32] In other words, duty and faithfulness must be continually reviewed and assessed in light of our past and our future. In the words of Abraham Lincoln, "...Let us to the end dare to do our duty as we understand it."[33]

The duty to our neighbor is part of our duty to God.[34] It is not the government's duty. It is my duty. It is your duty. Let's come before our Maker for clarification of our duties. One thing He has made clear is this, "It is required in stewards, that a man be found faithful."[35]

THE FIDELITY FULCRUM

The "fulcrum" is the point over which a lever is balanced. The position of the fulcrum determines whether the lever will be balanced, "all else being equal," as in a child's see-saw.

Fidelity to God's plans and design is the fulcrum over which the lever or see-saw of a man's, or nation's, life is balanced. If the fulcrum is out of "balanced" position, the see-saw is not in balance unless weight is added or adjustments are made to compensate. If the fulcrum is removed, there is no action possible—the lever cannot move, no matter how much weight is added.

That is a simple picture of our plight as a nation. God Himself has established the fulcrum. He has declared and ordained plans whereby we can prosper as individuals, families, and as a nation. But when we tamper with the fulcrum or attempt to relocate it to suit our desires, the lever of personal and national life does not balance. We then find ourselves trying to shore up one side or the other of life's see-saw to create balance. We do this by throwing tremendous quantities of time and money at our problems that result from our "infidelity" to the fulcrum.

Our Creator tried to make it simple. He stated in the Bible, "Let us hear the conclusion of the whole matter: Fear God, and keep his commandments, for this is the whole duty of man."[36]

View of Our Founding Fathers

The Mayflower Compact, signed as the Pilgrims were preparing to land on our eastern shore, clearly described the understanding of those Founding Fathers in coming to these shores:

> Having undertaken, for the glory of God and advancement of the Christian Faith and honor of our King and country, do by these presents solemnly and mutually in the presence of God and one another, covenant and combine ourselves into a civil body politic....[37]

The Puritan colony under the governorship of a lawyer, John Winthrop, was established by a similar document, entitled "A Model of Christian Charity." It stated:

> We are a company, professing ourselves fellow members of Christ, we ought to account ourselves knit together by this bond of love....

> Thus stands the cause between God and us: we are entered into covenant with Him for this work.[38]

These two colonies and their founders impacted American society, government, and law more than any other influences. They set the direction, the purpose, and the means for establishing the nation. Based upon those premises, this nation has become the greatest nation, not just in terms of power but for good in the history of mankind.

The founding principles were that of a covenant or promise:

First: There was declared a covenant between the founders and God Himself to honor, respect, and obey God's laws and commands for prosperous living.

Second: There was declared a covenant between the people to love, honor, care for, and respect one another issuing out of God's love, care, and respect for them.

The Plymouth and Puritan colonies set forth in good faith to honor those covenants. They developed laws based upon those covenants issuing straight from the Bible. Our present system of law is a byproduct of their covenants. When they erred and violated those covenants, they sought God's forgiveness and repented, always seeking to faithfully preserve their covenant with God. For they knew and had written into the founding document itself that if they were unfaithful to God's plan and call and to their observance of the covenant, "...the Lord will surely break out in wrath against us."[39]

View from the Parapets of History Today

As our Founding Fathers lean over the parapets of history to see the waywardness of the nation they "birthed," they must wrench in mortal terror for the wrath now being poured out upon us. Surely we do not have to repeat "ad nauseam" the dire social, economic, moral, and spiritual mess we are in. Surely we are not so numb, so naive, so callous, or so blind that we cannot see the cause and effect relationship of our moral and spiritual rebellion against our Creator and our desperate national crises. We have breached the covenant. We have been unfaithful. And God cannot bless and prosper us.

Under God or "Under the Gun"

As a nation we have always looked to and trusted God to be faithful, knowing He would be true to His Word. We have expressed that confidence in many ways:

In our "Pledge of Allegiance," we declare we are "One nation *under God,* indivisible..."

In *America the Beautiful*, America's favorite patriotic song, we sing, "America, America, God shed His grace on thee..."

In *My Country 'Tis of Thee* we sing: "Long may our land be bright, With freedom's holy light; Protect us by Thy might, Great God our king."

In our national anthem, The Star-Spangled Banner, we declare: "And this be our motto: *In God is our trust.*"

As a nation and a people, we have not hesitated to express our trust and our confidence in God as the ruler of nations and rewarder of them who diligently seek Him. One of the great gospel songs sung in our churches is *Great is Thy Faithfulness.* We know in our hearts that He is faithful. But we also know in our hearts that we are not.

In his book, *America's Only Hope*, a vibrant black pastor from Dallas, Texas, Dr. Tony Evans, boldly trumpets: "The problems we face in our society are the result of individuals, families, churches, and society at large making up new rules rather than following God's rules."[40]

Dr. Evans continues: "We must realize the serious nature of our covenant with God....When we fail to keep the terms of the covenant, it affects all other relationships as well."[41]

A Call to the Church

While this book is a letter to America at large, I want to give brief, specific focus to those who currently profess faith in Jesus Christ—the Christian church in America. Folks, we have left our first love. We have been prodigal in our ways. And we are accountable—not just to God but to our nation. As the apostle Peter announced in the New Testament, "The time is come that judgment must begin at the house of God."[42]

George Gallup, in a survey conducted among business executives and the general public for the *Wall Street Journal*, found "very little difference between the churched and the unchurched in terms of their general views on ethical matters, and also their practical ethical responses in various situations."[43]

That is a scathing indictment! What has happened to God's church in America since Alexis de Tocqueville declared in the first half of the nineteenth century, "Not until I went into the churches of America and heard her pulpits flame with righteousness did I understand the secret of her genius and power"?[44]

Quoting Dr. Tony Evans once again, we look at our responsibility in the church:

Since God is the source of the church's authority, He holds the church accountable to function according to His authority.[45]

If the church operates apart from His authority, God says He will withdraw His presence, leaving it powerless.[46]

Jesus is not smiling at the way we run our lives. He's not grinning at the way we run our homes. He's not happy about how we run our churches.[47]

Pastors must be absolutely sure that they **are** proclaiming Jesus' message to His church.[48]

As a pastor, I am also accountable for making sure God's people implement His message.[49]

Sermons are to declare the Word of God.[50]

God's Word cuts and prunes away.[51]

Everyone in the church is accountable to abide by the terms of the covenant—the pastor, the elders, the deacons, the whole congregation.[52]

If the church is ever to fulfill its mission, it must hold God's people accountable to Him.[53]

We are accountable for our actions to the Lord of the church.[54]

A Call to My Fellow Americans

Today is the day of reckoning. Today is the moment of decision. We must each, individually, humble ourselves, pray, repent of our errant and arrogant ways, so that we can once again be found faithful. And God will once again bless us.

An article in the seventy-fifth anniversary edition of *Forbes* remorsefully states, "People don't have faith in America's future anymore."[55] Restoring faith requires restoring fidelity. Fidelity or faithfulness is a sure cure for infidelity.

The Marine Corps motto is *"Semper Fidelis—*Always Faithful." No Marine can forget that motto. Let us all restore faithfulness in America—in our private lives, at our jobs, in our churches, in our families. Let it begin with me and you. In the words of a song, "May all who come behind us find us faithful."[56]

*Courage is
character in action.*

CHAPTER ELEVEN

Take Courage

THE TORCH OF TRUE FREEDOM is carried by the courageous living of men and women who dare to live a cut above the survival mentality of the masses. Such are men and women who choose the road of selfless service—who refuse to be sucked into the mire of despair about them. They re-light the lamp of liberty for us when they speak, when they act, and when we reminisce on their heroic deeds.

Most of our historic examples are not men or women of rank or noble birth. They are regulars in the army of life—just like you and me. You and I are called upon to take up the torch of freedom in our time. Let us, for our own encouragement, peek through the window of history at just a few profiles of courage from the annals of America's past.

PROFILES OF COURAGE

Molly Pitcher

On June 28, 1778, a hot battle broke out near the home of Mary Ludwig Hayes in Monmouth, New Jersey. Her husband, John, was a gunner. The thirty-four-year-old housewife helped the soldiers by drawing pitchers of water from a nearby spring. The soldiers began calling her "Molly Pitcher." When John Hayes fell, unable to man his cannon, Mary grabbed the rammer, reloaded, and began firing the cannon. In the process, a cannonball sailed between her legs, tearing away part of her petticoat. After the battle, General Washington called her, "Sergeant Molly."[1]

Crispus Attucks

On a snowy March 5, 1770, Crispus Attucks led a group of men into the Boston town square. Crispus had been a slave twenty years earlier. He opposed the British rule and the threat to colonial freedom. British soldiers had knocked down a young boy, and Boston's citizens were outraged. Crispus and other colonists, unarmed, faced the armed British Redcoats. Suddenly a rock was thrown by someone in the crowd and an order rang out, "Fire!" Crispus Attucks and four other colonists were killed in what came to be known as "The Boston Massacre." The brave death of those five courageous men inspired the colonists and continues to ring the bell of freedom two centuries later.[2]

Francis Scott Key

During the War of 1812, Francis Scott Key, a lawyer in his early thirties, agreed to take the responsibility to seek the release of Dr. William Beanes, who had been captured by the British in their invasion of Washington, D.C. The British had burned the White House, and President Madison and his wife, Dolly, had narrowly escaped.

Dr. Beanes was being held prisoner aboard a ship in the British fleet which was maneuvering in Chesapeake Bay to attack Baltimore. Francis Scott Key was taken out to the British fleet under a truce flag. After serious negotiations, the doctor's release was promised, but due to the British attack plan, Key was detained aboard the British fleet during the night while they bombarded Fort McHenry.

Caught in the midst of the cannon fire, he witnessed the vicious battle firsthand. His courageous act of care for the dear doctor, and his personal risk, put him in position to inspire the entire nation as he penned the words of our national anthem. The words of *The Star Spangled Banner* turned the hearts of a discouraged American people to victory in the War of 1812, and continue to stir the heart of every American today.[3]

Barbara Frietchie

When the advance troops of the Confederacy moved through Frederick, Maryland in 1862, most of the citizens locked up their homes and businesses and hauled in their Union flags. Not Barbara Frietchie. The ninety-seven-year-old widow defiantly went to the top of her house, leaned far out of her attic window, and waved the Stars and Stripes. Shots broke the flag staff, but the indomitable Barbara Frietchie fetched the flag and continued to wave it. Her memory was preserved and honored by John Greenleaf Whittier in his poem, *Barbara Frietchie*, giving us lasting insight into the spark of courage that her courageous act brought at a time of national turmoil.[4]

CONCEIVED IN COURAGE

They left England reluctantly, under great persecution. They were hounded, bullied, imprisoned on trumped-up charges, and driven underground—all because of their desire to sincerely worship God according to the dictates of their conscience. They were labeled "separatists" because they did not want to fall prey to the decay of English society. Their message was not "politically correct." They finally sought religious asylum in Holland, which cost them dearly.

A dozen years later, their children, worn by the lures of ungodly society in Holland, and the bodies of the adults having wasted under almost unbearable toil, their spirits were sparked by the hope of establishing a society in the New World—America— where religious, social, and political freedom could be established in covenantal relationship with each other under God.

As they boarded the *Mayflower* to sail for these shores, they were not ignorant of the difficulties that lay ahead. They heard of the tremendous death rate in Virginia from starving, of the savagery of the Indians, and the death rate at Jamestown. Yet, they also had a high calling and a firm purpose. With God's help and provision, they could make it.

Thus the Pilgrims embarked on a journey of great courage and bravery that brought them to Plymouth Rock in 1620. We would not have become the nation of greatness and glory revealed by the last 300 years were it not for the courageous conviction in the hearts and minds of the Pilgrims and the Puritans.

William Bradford, a leader of the Pilgrim expedition, and governor of that colony for thirty years, expressed the tremendous depth of their heart resolve:

It was answered that all great and honorable actions are accompanied with great difficulties, and must be enterprised and overcome with answerable courages. It was granted that the dangers were great, but not desperate, and the difficulties were many, but not invincible...and all of them, through the help of God, by fortitude and patience, might either be borne or overcome. Their ends were good and honorable...therefore, they might expect the blessing of God on their proceeding; Yea, though they should lose their lives in this action, yet they might have comfort in the same, and their endeavors would be honorable.[5]

BORN IN BRAVERY

On July 4, 1776, the Declaration of Independence was adopted. As president of the Continental Congress, John Hancock signed first, boldly and conspicuously. Knowing he laid his very life on the line, he declared, "There, I guess King George will be able to read that." The fifty-six patriots who affixed their names to that document of freedom declared solemnly, yet firmly, "...With a firm reliance on the protection of Divine Providence, we mutually pledge to each other our lives, our fortunes, and our sacred honor."

Samuel Adams, in writing to his wife of the momentous occasion, revealed his clear sense of courageous commitment:

I am well aware of the toil, and blood, and treasure that it will cost us to maintain this declaration.... I can see that the end is more than worth all the means, and that posterity will triumph in that day's transaction.[6]

On March 23, 1775, a few short months before the signing of the Declaration, Patrick Henry addressed the Virginia Convention with stirring words of courage and hope to which we might give renewed consideration amidst the great struggle we now face for survival as a nation. Listen to his thunder:

We are not weak if we make a proper use of those means which the God of Nature has placed in our power....

Besides, Sir, we shall not fight our battles alone. There is a just God who presides over the destinies of nations, who will raise up friends to fight our battles for us. The battle, Sir, is not to the strong alone; it is to the vigilant, the active, the brave.[7]

In his Phi Beta Kappa oration to Harvard University in 1953, Elmer Davis trumpeted a message we must hear: "This Republic was not established by cowards; and cowards will not preserve it."[8]

CONTRASTS IN COURAGE

The ship was sinking, a gaping hole in her hull. There was no hope of saving her. She would certainly make her resting place at the bottom of the sea. Passengers alerted to the plight paced the decks frantically. Others remained in their cabins—unaware at first of their desperate doom.

The captain and crew, however, sprang into action. They quickly and skillfully began to maneuver the lifeboats into the churning sea. And then the captain and crew made their way into the lifeboats, abandoning the doomed vessel—and her passengers.

Fortunately, the desperate plight of the sinking ship and her passengers reached the responsive ear of help from shore. Helicopters were dispatched, and one by one the stranded passengers were snatched from the jaws of certain death. After hours of the dramatic rescue effort, the last of the passengers having been saved, the ship slipped under the surface and out of sight.

As television watchers of the rescue later viewed the drama unfold in a TV special, they were gripped in suspense as the trapped passengers waited as patiently as humanly possible for their turn to escape the clutches of death. But the joy of heroic rescue was a mixed blessing for viewers as the pallor of cowardice of the defecting captain and crew hung over the story. The captain was arrested and prosecuted for abandoning his duty.

In contrast, one is immediately reminded of classical expressions of courage arising from the sea and our nation's past. "Don't give up the ship" was the battle cry inscribed on the flag flown from Oliver Hazzard Perry's ship in the Battle of Lake Erie on September 10, 1813.[9] On September 13, 1779, John Paul Jones, captain of the *Bonhomme Richard,* engaged the British frigate *Serapis* in battle at point-blank range. After daringly sailing directly against the British vessel, he locked the vessels together. During the fight, two of his cannons exploded. When the British captain called for surrender, Jones responded, "Sir, I have not yet begun to fight."[10]

While we revel in the daring and glory of such bravery and courage, and debase the cowardice of the captain who abandons his ship, it is easy to mask and lose sight of more fundamental issues of courage which impact us where we live. What do we do in our homes? How do we behave in our communities? What is my courage quotient? Have I abandoned ship?

A HAUNTING QUESTION

What is my duty?

Courage arises from a perception of responsibility, from a sense of duty. The problem is that when duty calls, some people are never at home. The greater the number of people who are "not home" when duty calls, the more apparent lack of courage becomes in our society.

Most of us remember the New York story emblazoned across the national news a few short years ago. Screams were heard in the neighborhood. It was clear a woman was in urgent need of help. The cry for help was heart-rending! But the terrified cry failed to rend any hearts that evening.

No, the cries did not go unheard. Many were drawn to their windows to see what was happening. And view they did, but none saw fit to respond to the woman's desperate plight, although well they could have.

Her death did not occur instantly. There was warning. There was time. There was opportunity to act as the attacker pursued his victim. But the onlookers looked on, mesmerized as if watching just another bloody movie. After all, they were warm, safe, and cozy in their homes and apartments. Why should they get involved? It did not affect them... at least not today. It wasn't their responsibility, was it? The deadly silence that followed gave loud testimony to the waning of courage in

140

American society. A woman lay dead in the street. One might ask whether her death was due to the viciousness of her attacker or to breach of duty of the onlookers. Whatever your view, it is evident that no bravery, no courage, lifted the American spirit that evening. The question remains, "What is my duty?"

THE CALL OF DUTY

Courage arises in response to the call of duty. But duty is no longer easily defined because we have done cultural violence to the sources from which duty flows.

Duty is defined in a much larger life context. It is defined first by the "authorities" in my life—parents, law, government, our civil institutions, the Church, and God Himself. To the extent I step out from under any authority in my life, I lose my sense of duty that arises from that relationship. If I step out from under God's authority, either by direct decision or by my behavior over time, I lose my sense of the duties that emanate from that relationship.

As I shed my allegiance to legitimate authority, I claim increasing rights while shedding corresponding responsibility. The result is that I serve only myself and have no obligations. Ultimately, even civil law itself becomes powerless to guide or establish my "bottom-line" duty, resulting in anarchy where courage is redefined to mean the ultimate service to myself rather than the ultimate service to others. When Patterson and Kim announce in *The Day America Told the Truth,* "You are the law in this country. Who says so? You do, pardner,"[11] they are decrying the very undermining of all authority that is gradually destroying our sense of duty. Courage pales into insignificance when not even the law will get my attention.

But there is another critical context for the seeds of courage to grow and prosper. That context is society itself. A sense of duty becomes the call of duty only if I perceive myself in genuine, valuable relationship to those around me—my spouse, children, church, neighborhood, and even my country.

What happens if I lose that sense of value in the various levels of social and cultural relationship about me? What if the only thing that really matters is "economics" rather than moral and spiritual values which require the investment of mind and heart with others and with my God? I become what is now being described by sociologists and astute observers an "economic man."

The "economic man" does not work to live, but lives to work. He is not necessarily a workaholic but finds life's meaning in his work and the financial economy he creates, rather than in the relationships about him. Relationships serve his economy rather than his economy serving the relationships. And in the process, he is increasingly alienated from both God and man. He is becoming "independent."

Such is the current condition of American life today. To one degree or another, we have all been affected. We have become increasingly alienated from one another. In our desire to be independent, we have lost an essential dependence that is required for meaningful living. We are rapidly speeding toward that place where we declare our independence from God and man. If we reach that point as a nation, we are doomed. If I reach that point as an individual citizen, I am, at best, most miserable. If you and I are on that path, we are dying a slow death.

In such an environment of alienation and isolation, courage cannot take root. "Alienation! Isolation! Individualism! Anarchism!..." warns Richard Halverson, Chaplain of the United States Senate in his April 22, 1992, issue of *Perspective*, are the "door to Tyranny."[12] Relationship and authority comprise the soil in which duty grows, producing the fruit of courage, which rises against tyranny of any sort. Yes, even the tyranny of crime and drugs in the streets of your city will succumb to the courage of neighbors and local citizens who see themselves bound in relationship with each other.

We can courageously make a difference *together*—in relationship with God and each other. We are in this together. Do we have what it takes? If not, can we get it back? Can we restore courage to the American soul?

THE AMERICAN BACKBONE

When the authors of *The Day America Told the Truth* inquired in their poll about what beliefs people would die for, forty-eight percent said "none." Only thirty percent would be willing to die for God and their faith under any circumstances. Even fewer, twenty-four percent, would die for their country. They observe, "Americans of the 1990s stand alone in a way unknown to any previous generation."[13] These, they say, are the "measure of Americans' alienation from the traditional authority of God and country."[14] Such is the observation of secular analysts. "We've become wishy-washy as a nation," they conclude. "Some would say that we've lost our moral backbone."[15]

RESTORING THE MORAL BACKBONE

The famous sage, Goethe, left us with words well worth our serious personal consideration:

> Wealth lost, something lost;
> Honor lost, much lost;
> Courage lost, all lost.[16]

Courage is the backbone of moral character. When courage weakens, the back slumps. When courage leaves, the back is broken. The moral back of America is slumping seriously. Yet the moral back of a nation is built upon the moral fiber of its people. There is no national morality without personal morality. And there is no national courage without personal courage. Unfortunately, much of what passes as courage these days is poured from a bottle or popped as a pill. As James Michaels observed in his article, "Oh, Our Aching Angst," published in *Forbes*, September 14, 1992, "It isn't the economic system that needs fixing.... It's our value system."[17]

Courage is inextricably linked to all aspects of character and moral behavior. One can barely fathom leadership without courage. Is it any wonder we languish for leadership? Consider honesty. Can honesty prevail in the absence of moral courage to deliver the truth? Or consider fidelity. It takes courage these days to resist the rising tide of infidelity in all areas of life. The simple truth is that courage links all of character and morality into a single operative body that enables a man or woman to "take a stand."

TAKING A STAND

Are you willing to take a stand? If willing, are you *ready* to take a stand? Given the condition of your moral backbone, are you in any condition to take a stand? Or will the winds of social pressure, employment compromise, relational infidelity, and selfish ambition topple your feeble moral frame? Do you even have something to stand for? Is it worth standing for? Why?

If you don't stand for something, you'll fall for anything. Be bold in what you stand for, but be careful in what you fall for.

In this world of "political correctness," it is dangerous to check the prevailing winds before determining your stand on any issue or matter. Morality is not determined by majority rule. Neither is truth established by the strident voice of a vocal minority. If we have lost "common" sense, we cannot have a common consensus. I must be willing to search for and speak the truth—even if I must stand alone.

THE COURAGE OF CONSCIENCE

Courage is forged in the crucible of conscience. Where there is no conscience, courage languishes. Where the conscience is seared through violation or is twisted through "political correctness," courage has a hollow and uncertain ring. "Conscience in the soul is the root of all true courage," reflected J. F. Clarke. "If a man would be brave, let him learn to obey his conscience."[18]

Where there is no conscience, the moral and spiritual fabric of life has become threadbare. If we wish to see a refreshing rise of courage in American life, business, and politics, we must first reweave the moral and spiritual fabric of our society. That does not begin with my neighbor or my congressman. It begins with me.

The call of courage in our society in these United States as we approach the twenty-first century is enough for more than a few good men. "When moral courage feels that it is in the right, there is no personal daring of which it is incapable," said Leigh Hunt.[19] Your courage quotient is a direct reflection of your conscience quotient. So what is your conscience quotient?

William Bentley Ball, a constitutional attorney of renown, in his editorial comments prefacing *In Search of a National Morality,* winces in commenting, "Moral courage [is] that most unfashionable virtue."[20] In the same collection of essays, Paul C. Vitz, professor of psychology at New York University, observes, "America has now reached the point where it permits almost everything and stands for almost nothing—except flabby relativism."[21]

What do you stand for? If it feels good, do you do it? If it suits your present need, do you modify your principles? Are you a man or woman of principle? Do you exercise restraint in the face of your desires?

Courage is not much needed to do what I want but rather to do what I ought. If I would see courage arise in America, I must break the paralysis of fear that renders me a moral wimp. It is a choice. Your choice and mine will determine America's survival. George Washington, in his "Farewell Address," rhetorically and yet prophetically asks, "Can it be, that Providence has not connected the permanent felicity of a Nation with its virtue?"[22]

THE CALL TO COURAGE

Slavery was not a new issue when our sixteenth president was sworn into office. It had been an issue of moral confrontation in the American mind and heart for a century. But it had been presented acutely to the American conscience by such spokesmen as the lawyer-turned-preacher, Charles Finney, in the years before 1860 in the confluence of moral and spiritual revival in the nation.

Slavery was not just a moral issue in the abstract. It permeated every aspect of the social and economic structure of an entire region within the nation. While its continued presence was unconscionable, its eradication was unpalatable to the entire South. There were no easy answers. There was no way to act on the issue or fail to act without making enemies.

Such was the heritage of Abraham Lincoln at his inauguration. His Emancipation Proclamation made him a moral hero to some and a political and social reject to others. His memory is a tribute to his great courage, for he ranks with our founding president, George Washington, in the hearts of Americans. In his famous "Gettysburg Address," we get insight into the foundation for his courage and for the basis for his hope for a restored nation. His words continue to ring 150 years later:

"This nation, under God, shall have a new birth of freedom..."[23]

THE COST OF COURAGE

While courage is the backbone of our personal and national character, courage is not without cost. There is a price to be paid in acquiring courage. To obtain courage, I must sacrifice self and personal ambition on the altar of service. I must dispel fear with faith. And I must pursue truth and justice rather than "political correctness."

There is also a cost in being courageous. Lincoln lost friends...then his life. A century later when he announced, "I have a dream," Dr. Martin Luther King was not living in dreamland. He knew there was a price for liberty as captured in the words of Thomas Payne, "That which is bought too cheaply is esteemed too lightly."[24] His courage to confront injustice in the entire social order cost him dearly. He paid with his life. His courage issued out of his faith.

The fifty-six signers of our Declaration of Independence counted the cost in pledging "our lives, our fortunes, and our sacred honor."

Freedom is the sure possession only of those who have the courage to defend it. There is no freedom without truth, without justice. Freedom is not free. What is it worth to you? Do you have the courage to defend it? Will you defend it? At what cost?

Consider your *courage* being expressed actively this week in:

- Courage of *conscience*, to do what is right.
- Courage to *conform*, to do what the law requires of you.
- Courage to *change*, to change your own thinking.
- Courage to *communicate*, to speak on issues of importance.
- Courage to *consider*, to rethink preconceived notions.
- Courage to *care*, to take personal responsibility for others and your nation.
- Courage to *confront*, to stand up to untruth and injustice.
- Courage to *challenge*, to change the way we've always done it, if wrong.
- Courage to *correct*, to change my own behavior if wrong.

• Courage to *confess*, to acknowledge my personal wrongs toward others, my lack of courage, and my sin and rebellion toward God.

Don't be afraid to go out on a limb if the limb is worthy. That's where the fruit is.

CULTIVATING COURAGE

As light becomes known in darkness, so courage manifests itself in the waning light of moral, spiritual, social, and political strife, turmoil, and decay. When darkness and discouragement abound, the light of courage pierces the darkness, radiating to the unseen extremities of the blackness that surrounds us. It carries on its wings a message of hope. It reveals an unseen dimension beyond the pain of the present.

But courage cannot be merely "mustered" from one's own bootstraps. We wish it were so, but such is not the usual tale of history. "This is the way to cultivate courage," said J. F. Clarke, "first, by standing firm on some conscientious principle, some law of duty. Next, by being faithful to truth and right on small occasions and common events. Third, by trusting God for help and power."[25]

Cicero told us, "A man of courage is also full of faith."[26] We must, as Americans, humble ourselves before God so we can be in position to receive His faith and the courage which naturally flows. "It takes more courage for us to repent than to keep on sinning."[27] If we will repent, turn, and decide once again to cooperate with God's plan and purposes as did our Founders, we will once again see the return of courage in our land. And while we stand trembling, "prayer gives strength to the weak, faith to the fainthearted, and courage to the fearful."[28] The Bible tells us, "Men ought always to pray, and not to faint."[29]

TAKE COURAGE

"On many of the great issues of our time, men have lacked wisdom because they have lacked courage," declared William Benton.[30] We have certainly experienced both lack of wisdom and lack of courage in our national life. It has resulted in a sense of aimlessness—a feeling of lack of direction. But we need no longer wander in trepidation and fear. We must take courage.

Courage is "taken" as we appropriate underlying truth or substance upon which courage can be based. Courage must be based on solid ground and not on the fleeting fancies of men's minds.

I was given the opportunity of obtaining an original page of a volume of the first printing of the King James version of the Bible, published in 1611. The entire Bible was no longer intact. I had a choice of several pages, and I chose the title page for the Book of Joshua, which I have mounted on my office wall. I think it is most fitting to conclude this chapter with a quotation from God's own directive for success and courage at such a time as this.

This book of the law shall not depart out of thy mouth; but thou shalt meditate therein day and night, that thou mayest observe to do according to all that is written therein: for then thou shalt make thy way prosperous, and then thou shalt have good success....

Be strong and of a good courage; be not afraid, neither be thou dismayed: for the Lord thy God is with thee whithersoever thou goest.[31]

Is God with you? Are you with Him? If so, take courage. If you have breached relationship with Him, turn right now, determine to follow God's way, and then do it. Courage will once again rise in your heart.

The next generation is depending on you. Based upon your courage quotient, what is America's future? What is the future of your family? It is your courageous example that will make a difference. Take courage.

There is no national faith
without personal faith.

CHAPTER TWELVE

Faith and Freedom

IT WAS THE DARKEST HOUR of the American Revolution. By mid-December, 1777, there were but eleven thousand men remaining in the ranks of the Continental Army. They had just completed a daring attack on the British at Germantown and had suffered heavy losses.

Desertion was a serious problem. Troops were weary and their clothing torn and tattered. Blankets were scarce and shoes even scarcer. It was only a month earlier, on Thanksgiving Day, that Lieutenant Colonel Henry Dearborn wrote of the American army, "...God knows we have little to keep it with, this being the third day we have been without flour or bread."[1] Food could have been plentiful, but the civilians often hoarded it, and transporting it was difficult.

The Continental Congress then governing the colonies had just adopted the Articles of Confederation, a weak and toothless document purporting to join the colonies but giving little support to the marshaling and support of troops. Patting themselves on the back for their labors, most of the Continental Congress went home for Christmas, closing their eyes to the plight of the army they claimed to support.

But General Washington could not close his eyes. He was responsible for men who had staked their lives, their fortunes, and their sacred honor on his leadership. Amidst criticism, he chose to gather his troops together for the winter rather than to risk another attack and certain defeat in their weakened condition. So it was that they set up camp twenty miles from Philadelphia, at a place whose memory is embedded with pain in the memory of every American—a place called Valley Forge.

As they dragged themselves to Valley Forge, Washington said, "...you might have tracked the army from White March to Valley Forge by the blood of their feet."[2] And things there did not improve. Shelter was meager, at best. Amidst snow and biting cold, they bound their feet in rags as they built huts and lugged water on a two-mile round trip for survival. But many did not survive. Starvation, nakedness, cold, and disease claimed the lives of 2,600 troops.[3]

In this test of mettle, General Washington remained the "General" to his men. It was not his title but his tough, yet tender tenacity of inner strength and character that held his troops, that preserved their resolve and gave them endurance. He seemed to draw strength, direction, and purpose from a wellspring not found in the soil of Valley Forge but from the soil of his own heart. And indeed he did.

In that darkest hour, Washington the general drew upon his faith in God. His was not a "foxhole" faith but a faith borne of long-standing relationship to his God. He knew the source of his strength and of his ability to lead. He knew that true leadership stems from humility—humility before one's Maker. He knew he was a servant, and that the "Ruler of Nations" was the Supreme Commander.

And he bowed his knee and his heart in humble service to the King of kings. Washington's private faith has been publicly memorialized for all Americans in the famous painting depicting him kneeling in prayer in the Valley Forge snow. His prayerful image is further memorialized in stained glass in the chapel just off the rotunda of the United States Capitol.

But the personal faith of Washington was also memorialized in the lives of his troops. Whether they individually accepted his God we cannot attest, but one thing is certain—they honored and respected their general for his own steady faith in God, and received the blessings of that faith in his leadership.

On Washington's death in 1799, a former cavalry officer, Henry Lee of Virginia, who had become a member of the House of Representatives, honored Washington by declaring him "...first in war, first in peace, and first in the hearts of his countrymen."[4]

Perhaps the words of John Marshall, one of America's greatest Supreme Court Chief Justices, best conveys the spirit of Washington's faith: "Without making ostentatious professions of religion, he was a sincere believer in the Christian faith and a truly devout man."[5] "To Christian institutions he gave the countenance of his example."[6]

In the fury of life's battlefields, which are many, godly faith will always form the foundation of freedom. The hope of true freedom, without godly faith, is futility.

NOT GLORY BUT GRACE

The filtered eye of history reflects the "glory" of the American Revolution. Acts of bravery and the spirit of patriotism ride high in our memory. As the bell of freedom rings in our hearts, we rejoice and savor that moment in our history which gave rise to the precious blessings of liberty we now enjoy.

But the American Revolution was not a "moment" for those whose lives were wrapped in its fury. It was the light of freedom being hammered out in the crucible of faith. Time and again the colonial troops were faced with overwhelming odds against them. The crack British Redcoats were a well-oiled, well-financed war machine that ruled the seas and were the preeminent military power of the day. Yet account after account of victory against odds and protection against annihilation revealed the increasing truth that it was not by men's glory but by God's grace that America was born as an independent nation.

Freedom was born in the womb of God's grace through men of faith who were faithful. Washington himself, in his first inaugural address, publicly gave recognition to this fact.

"No People can be bound to acknowledge and adore the invisible hand, which conducts the Affairs of men more than the People of the United States."[7]

Neither time nor space in this book will permit recounting

153

the details of how God, in His divine grace and mercy, repeatedly protected the colonial troops, caused dense fogs to fall and rise at critical moments, caused confusion among the British, and rendered enemy leadership directionless and inert at moments of greatest vulnerability to the fighters for freedom.

OUR VALLEY FORGE

America is in desperate need for the intervention of the invisible hand of the Ruler of Nations at this dark hour of our nation's history. Freedom is at stake. We need a resurgence of true *faith* in this critical hour. We do not need faith in faith. That is mere bootstrapping. We need a mighty awakening in our hearts and souls of faith in the God who rules and governs in the affairs of men. We need a personal faith, a faith that can stand against the tide of the tyranny of "political correctness" and the stripping of moral absolutes from our personal and national wardrobe.

We are in our own Valley Forge. As Americans who believe in the cause of true freedom under God, we have become weary, have lost direction, our feet are bloodied, our moral and spiritual clothes are tattered, and we have been on a spiritual starvation diet. We are weakened. Many of us have died morally and spiritually—even in our churches.

We need *faith* in America. Again, the faith we need in this land is not faith in faith, nor is it a patriotically inspired, bootstrapped, emotionally hyped faith in America, but faith in the God who preserved us a nation. We cannot look to a charismatic leader, we cannot wait for a euphoric uprising of "good feelings" from another Gulf War. We need faith in God Almighty...and we need it *now*!

But there is no national faith without personal faith. The question is not whether my neighbor has faith, or the president, or my congressman, or even my pastor or priest. The question is whether I am a man or woman of faith. Have I put my personal faith and trust in my Creator? Am I yielded to Him and to His will? Or have I become part of the problem? Am I faithless? Have I gradually turned my faith in God to faith in myself, in man's inventions, in the government, in education, in anything or anyone but the Most High God? We can see the wasteland of that kind of "faith" all around us. Let's take another look.

FAITH WASTELAND

Charles Colson, former "hatchet man" for the Nixon administration and redeemed by the grace of God from the pit of Watergate and self-exaltation, has become a true statesman to America generally, but even more specifically to the professing Christian church in America. In his book, *The Body*, he writes with characteristic poignancy to those of us who claim to be called by the name of Christ as Christians. He states that we have developed a "McChurch" mentality, flitting about in search of what makes us *feel* good rather than in search of a faith that is rooted and grounded in substance.[8]

We have grown to love the froth rather than the faith. We run hither and yon in search of "What's in it for me?" And we have lost the substance of the faith we purport to embrace. Self-support has replaced self-denial. Love of self has replaced love of God. And American society careens off into faithlessness.

Men and women search for a tailor-made "god"—a god made in their own image, custom-shaped to their perception of what they want or think they need. It is no longer what I owe to my God, but what my God owes me. In such an environment of "I-ism," we no longer bear responsibility. We no longer need forgiveness of *sin*, for we only make "mistakes." We are a product of our environment, of a dysfunctional family, of too little, too much, too late. And life careens off into a wasteland, an endless and tumultuous sea where there are no absolutes suitable for anchor, no compass with which to gain perspective, and no maps with which to chart direction.

We are plunging recklessly and almost frantically ever deeper into the faith wasteland, the wilderness where there is no chart or compass, yet oblivious to where we are headed. All this at a time when pollsters talk about the continued significant presence of religion in America, liberals cry about the political power of the "Religious Right," and Bible-believing Christians fight to preserve the remaining vestiges of religious freedom provided by the First Amendment. How can we make sense of this confusion? How can we gain some perspective to sort out truth from fiction? And what is the impact of all of this in our lives and in the life of our nation?

TELLING STATISTICS

"Overall, sixty-four percent of the adults in America believe they are religious," says George Barna in his 1991 report titled *What Americans Believe*. This is a decline from seventy-two percent in 1985. Since nine out of ten senior citizens describe themselves as religious, it is easy to see what has happened to the younger generation; traditional religious commitment has dropped off dramatically, although a new trend is developing which we will look at in a moment.[9] Barna also reports that "two-thirds of all adults either agree strongly (twenty-two percent) or somewhat (forty-four percent) that America is a Christian nation."[10] One-third (thirty-four percent) of all adults classify themselves as "born-again" Christians.[11] And ninety percent of Americans say they believe in God.[12]

"God is alive and very well," declares authors Patterson and Kim in *The Day America Told the Truth*, "But right now in America, fewer people are listening to what God has to say than ever before."[13] That's quite a statement coming from two advertising executives! Apparently, it is not God who has changed, but Americans. A couple of years ago, as our family was graciously hosted in one of Mississippi's finest ante-bellum plantations, our attention was attracted to a little plaque which we now display in our own home. The words seem appropriate here: "If you don't feel close to God, guess who moved?"

As Americans, we have gradually strayed from our faith in God and from our commitment to His purposes in our individual lives, in our families, in our communities, and even in our churches. One of the primary reasons for this increasing estrangement has been our redefining the laws or center of truth.

To our Founding Fathers, it was essentially a foregone conclusion that the Bible was the center and source of all ultimate truth. The Bible was the most quoted source in all of the writings of our Founding Fathers, and it was from that platform of dependable, unwavering truth that they announced to the world the American experiment in representative democracy—a republic—promising liberty and justice for all.

Without absolute confidence—faith—in the truth and authority of the Bible as the faithful expression of the Truth and

156

will of God, the American experiment of a democratic republic was foolhardy at best. It was the difference in foundation...the difference in faith...the difference in world view which made possible even the concept of a government of, by, and for the people. And it was the confidence of our Founders in the truth of the Christian way, based upon the Bible, that fueled the fires of the American Revolution...giving birth to a nation pursuing liberty and justice for all. As Noah Webster so aptly stated, "The religion which has introduced civil liberty is the religion of Christ and His apostles...to this we owe our free constitution of government."[14]

But now, as we stand tall in our national pride, we have dismissed that Divine Friend as only remotely relevant and have decided we can pick and choose that portion of His truth that patronizes our personal feelings and predilections. The source of truth is no longer fixed and dependable but varies with every personal whim and cultural shift. And as culture shifts, almost daily with the vagaries of human passion and prejudice, so our new comprehension of truth shifts, continually being redefined to serve the mandate of the moment. We have in fact so eroded, corroded, and "outmoded" our foundation as to be left with virtually no foundation at all. And faith is floundering...yes, yours and mine too, dear professing Christian, believe it or not. Together we have been cut loose on this sea of relativity, and we are in desperate need of catching a glimpse of light from God's "lighthouse"—the truth from a God who does not change with every vacillation of human experience...a truth that can steer us clear of the looming shoals of personal and national destruction.

It is most disheartening that sixty-three percent of all adult Americans have come to believe there is no such thing as absolute truth—truth that remains constant, relevant, and applicable throughout the changes and shifts in life's experiences and culture. Among even those claiming to be "born again," evangelical Christians, fifty-three percent believe there is no absolute, dependable truth upon which to base one's life, behavior, and decisions. Shockingly, seventy-three percent of mainline Protestants reject absolute truth.[15] Folks, that means that among Americans in mainline Protestant churches today, ten percent fewer believe in absolute truth than in the population at large. Clearly, no portion of the American populace

escapes the sinister blight of unbelief and faithlessness...
whether professing Christian or non-Christian. Yet it was the
firm conviction that God's truth, as expressed in the Bible, is
fully dependable for personal and national life and practice that
formed the very foundation of our nation. It should therefore
come as no surprise that we now flounder in heavy seas at
every level of society—both individually and institutionally.

We now run frantically to and fro in search of surrogate
truth. Having rejected absolute truth upon which we could build
our lives and preserve a nation, we search for and pursue a
plethora of "therapeutic" remedies to make us feel better and
help us cope. But it still isn't working. We seek therapy rather
than truth. The consequences are enormous—not just for
American society but for you, for me, and for our children and
grandchildren. We are all caught, to one degree or another, in
the swirling waters of unbelief and its consequences.

"As we entered the 1990s, it became suddenly and urgently
clear that a tumultuous change was occurring in America.... On
every front...the ground beneath our feet began shifting.
Yesterday's verities had vanished. Unpredictability and chaos
became the norm," declared advertisers Patterson and Kim.[16]
"We can no longer tell right from wrong," they observed. "It
raises fear and doubt which often leads to depression....
Americans in the 1990s have more of both fear and doubt—and
of depression, too—than did any previous generation....
Americans wrestle with these questions in what often amounts
to a moral vacuum. The religious figures and Scriptures that
gave us rules for so many centuries, the political system that
gave us our laws, all have lost their meaning in our moral imagination."[17] If it takes secular advertising executives to sound the
alarm, so be it. Somebody must tell the truth.

How Did it Happen?

So then, how did we get to this point? How did we lose our
moral backbone and our spiritual moorings? How did we discard truth and become faithless? Neither time nor space here
permit a thorough analysis of the scope and depth of these
questions, for they reach deep into our minds, hearts, and history; but we should at least take a brief look.

The Prosperity Pinch

As a nation, we have enjoyed fifty years of perpetual prosperity since World War II. True, there have been cycles where we experienced recession. Some areas of the country have experienced greater prosperity than others, and all families have not prospered equally. But for the most part, as a people we have certainly reaped the "blessings of liberty."

Prosperity carries with it a sense of "resting on our laurels." The principles and faith we cling to in climbing out of the pit of adversity we gradually relinquish as we mount the high road of prosperity. Most of us do not relinquish our faith and our principles with calculated intention, neither do we do it instantly. It is a gradual process. It occurs almost imperceptibly, until we look back and see how far we have strayed.

And we have definitely strayed over the last fifty years...more than a little. In fact, if we relied upon our faith level today to restart our personal, family, community, and national engines, many of us would not even get a response as we turned the key; others of us would get a brief turnover and nothing more; and a few would start, sputter, and succumb to silence. And that is true even of a large portion of churchgoers and Bible-toters. We have become weak in spirit. We don't want to admit it, and some of us may even argue and dispute it, but it is nevertheless true. For the spirit is fueled by faith, and we have run out of fuel.

It is a strange paradox that the very prosperity we seek and grasp for contains within it the seeds of decline and decay. It is not that prosperity is evil or wrong in itself. It is that we humans are not consistent. We become lax. And we become faithless. We place our lives on "cruise control" and forget to look at where the road is taking us until we realize we do not like the destination we have reached.

That is precisely where we find ourselves at this moment in American history—lost and without a compass. We feel it in the pit of our stomach. It is unnerving. And so our national headlines cry out, "Why We're So Gloomy,"[18] "The Glooming of America—A Nation Down in the Dumps,"[19] and "How Our American Dream Unraveled."[20] And we desperately grasp for solutions, hope, anything that will make us *feel* better. But we

159

don't feel better because our problem is not our feelings...it's our faith. Will our present adversity once again turn our hearts to faith? Will we—you, and I—again let God into our life...on His terms rather than ours? The choice is ours.

The Darkness of Enlightenment

I recently stood before a judge in a Southern California family law court, arguing a child-custody case on behalf of a client. Fortunately, there was little doubt as to which parent had shown consistent parental care and concern. There was also little doubt as to which parent demonstrated a faithful, consistent, and moral lifestyle. These observations were openly acknowledged by the court, so I won't "beat my own drum" here, or even that of my client. That is not why my thoughts are drawn to this incident.

One would think under such circumstances that the choice would have been clear and the court's decision easy. But no. Just as I expected to hear the court confirm custody to my client, I was shocked to "reality" as the judge ordered a "psychological evaluation" for the parties. "A psychological evaluation," I thought out loud. "This is not a case for a psychological evaluation!" To which the judge responded, "We live in an enlightened society," and then began to reflect on why we must rely upon the true wisdom of our society residing in the minds of psychotherapists.

You see, my client was a Christian minister whose teenage children dearly loved him. They had planned and considered as a family for nearly a year to move to another state because of their concern over the living environment for their family. The teenage son and daughter had, with heartfelt conviction, conveyed their own minds and hearts to the court, believing their faith and moral environment to be of greater value than pursuing friends, fortune, and fine living. These teenagers actually had a personal faith, personal convictions, and personal standards. They were prepared to leave the state.

How could this be? How could they cast away the "opportunities" of southern California so lightly? Surely something *is* wrong! We must have an enlightened psychologist look into this matter. And so they did.

I ask you to probe the inner recesses of your mind and heart.

Are we, indeed, living in an "enlightened" society? If so, why has almost every aspect of our society declined? Why do we have such perversion? Why has murder, rape, and other crime escalated to frightening proportions? Why does the drug culture have us in a "headlock" that defies the best efforts of law enforcement? Why do we lie to one another? Why can't we find leadership that we can depend on? Why are we—you, your relatives, your friends and neighbors—in frantic pursuit of therapy?

Out of France near the time of our own Revolutionary War came the seeds of the "Enlightenment." The theorists of the "Enlightenment" said that if we really want progress and true freedom, we must cast off the shackles of all that would bind us—tradition, faith, and family. France suffered as a result of this philosophy and has never truly recovered. Our Founding Fathers resisted it even though it was the avant-garde philosophy of the day. Our Founders realized it was a religion itself—of anti-faith. But this secular philosophy has now crept in and infected the minds of our entire society to one degree or another—even in the church. And as the American mind turned, so turned the American heart.

As I conversed with a publisher about publishing this book, he told me a story of a recent trip to Russia. He had been invited to present ways of providing Christian literature and materials for use in Russian schools. Russian leaders were literally crying out for Bibles and materials to help restore and build a spiritual base in a society that had been officially stripped of faith and family...and which had finally collapsed for want of a sure foundation.

One of the Russian leaders asked this publisher, "Could you use these materials in your schools in America today?" Sheepishly and in embarrassment, the publisher responded, "No, not in America today." Suddenly the Russian leader became obviously angry. In Russian, he began talking rapidly, raising his voice and pointing at the publisher. The publisher was taken aback, wondering how he had offended, and inquired of the interpreter. The words of that Russian leader, as related by the interpreter, should pierce the heart of every American: "Why is America doing this to itself? Can't you see that is what happened in Russia? Can't you see it doesn't work?"

Have we become "too big for our britches"? Do we really

know better? Or are we on a collision course with a "reality" we don't wish to experience? I think we are already beginning to experience that reality. Its statistics weigh us down with horror and despair. We are not "enlightened." Our foolish hearts have been darkened. But it is not too late to turn.

Did the God who made us and set the universe in its course go off on an eternal vacation? Or does He still have something to say to Americans who will humble themselves, turn from their self-exalted ways, and seek His wisdom and His righteousness? Can we afford this blind pursuit of philosophized and psychologized "enlightenment" that leads us down an ever-darkening path? Will we, like two-year-olds, continue to put our hands over our faces and say, "Look, God, you can't see me!"?

The judge in our custody case did finally grant custody to that father who chose to lead his family in faith. He also permitted those teenage children to follow their father in pursuit of a life and environment that would enable them to preserve and define a life of moral absolutes issuing out of personal faith. But the court's decision was not based upon the genuine life substance of that family which had enabled them to ride above the tumultuous tide of the society around them.

Following presentation of the psychological evaluation, the court invited final argument. I recounted factually and with passion the stability of that family—of the respect the children had for their father, of their unifying faith, of their moral and spiritual convictions, of their mutual desire to seek a living environment to foster moral purity and family stability, and of a desire to see all these borne out in their continued education. To which the court responded, "Mr. Crismier, the court is interested in things related to the best interests of these children, and I have not yet heard you address these matters."

A lawyer is seldom without words, but I was speechless, dumbfounded. To my mind, I had just recounted and touched upon the most foundational and substantive issues that could affect the lives those children. Already established to the court's satisfaction were employment, housing, extended family availability, and schooling. And so, in frustration, I inquired what information the court could possibly consider as "essential" to the best interests of the children that had not been presented. The court's response reflects, I believe, the shallowness of "enlightenment" thinking and its hopelessness in presenting any redeeming social or other value to American society. The court proceeded to ask for availability of "enrichment" activities: sports, music lessons, youth activities.

What a commentary on America life and values! And I thought of parents of hundreds, if not thousands, of families I had encountered in my eighteen years of law practice—families disintegrating, full of activities but void of active faith, running fast and furious to provide "enrichment" to mind and body but impoverishing soul and spirit. I recalled young children longing for time with mom while being rushed from ballet lessons to Girl Scouts to flute lessons, while mother got her nails painted so she would feel good enough about herself to spend her weekly hour with her therapist, to try to find some meaning in her treadmill existence.

I thought of fathers who were too tired to take their families to church by 9:30 Sunday morning but could be regularly found on the golf course by 7:00 a.m. And of fathers who worked six or seven days a week to provide a car for their sons on their sixteenth birthdays while having provided those sons with no sense of moral responsibility or understanding of how to provide moral or spiritual leadership to their own family. And I thought of "Christian" families where dad's behavior and values on Monday bear no relationship to dad's "profession" on Sunday at church; and where mom's interests and conversation on Tuesday sounds strangely foreign to her hour of glossy show from 11:00 to noon in the Sunday morning service. I thought of the inner noise of clanging dissonance and hypocrisy of life and practice reverberating in the minds and hearts of America's children, numbing their sensibilities and cauterizing their moral and spiritual perception, leaving them with "enlightened" minds and darkened spirits—having no sense of their own reason for living, of ultimate value or purpose, or of how to get there. And they call this "enlightenment."

May God help us...and He will if we will let Him. Otherwise, the darkness of "enlightenment" will engulf us. For if the light that is in us be darkness, how great is that darkness! True enlightenment with which to preserve a nation issues from truth...truth that does not vary with my every whim or desire or with every new idea pumped into the world of thought by armchair philosophers bent on "freeing" us from the truth that will make us free.

Jesus Christ made the matter abundantly clear when He declared, "If ye continue in my word...ye shall know the truth, and the truth shall make you free."[21] Whose word will you believe? Our Founders chose to believe the Scriptures, and on that foundation built us a nation. On what foundation will you preserve us a nation?

A Chameleon Church

The primary resource for faith in society is the corporate body of Christian believers. This has been true in America since our forebears first set foot on these shores. Those individual Christian believers may belong or associate together in a variety of local churches which, if Protestant, may belong to denominations or which may be independent. Regardless of doctrinal focuses that may distinguish between various individuals, local churches, or denominations, the central doctrine remains the same—man is essentially sinful, he needs a savior, and Jesus Christ is the Savior. The source of that doctrine is the Bible, and Christians, historically, have been committed to the Bible as ultimate truth for life and practice.

From the landing of the Pilgrims in 1620 and of the Puritans, the Christian church and individual Christian believers have been the guiding light of the nation. Our national vision and purpose was Christian and was, as stated in the Mayflower Compact, to advance the Christian faith on these shores.[22] The mind of those early settlers was unswerving commitment to Christ and His gospel of salvation to everyone who would believe. The heart of those settlers was denial of self in service to Christ and to their fellow citizens as unto Christ. That was America, in principle and practice, for her first two hundred years. While not all Americans professed Christ as Savior, virtually all Americans accepted the Bible and its principles as foundational for successful living and government.

These facts were so open and obvious that the Frenchman, Alexis de Tocqueville, in his book, *Democracy in America*, stated, "Not until I went into the churches of America and heard her pulpits flame with righteousness did I understand the secret of her genius and power."[23] That book was written in the mid-1800s.

Today, 160 years later, America's "genius" is in question and her power is waning. People around the world increasingly "raise their eyebrows" at the nation that once stood for faith...and virtue...and honor, as they watch America's internal decay and the increasing fomentation of American society at every measurable level. Could it be that there is a clear connection between America's churches today and the decline of America's genius and power? A few brief observations will have to suffice in response.

First, America's pulpits no longer flame with righteousness. The pulpits, instead, either flame with political rhetoric to patronize the political predilections of those in the pews; or they pander to the "felt needs" of people seeking psychological therapy in religious garb and rhetoric to help them cope with life's struggles, created largely because they refuse to accept God's standards on God's terms. The messages emanating from America's pulpits preach a gospel of self-help rather than a gospel of salvation. We are creating a custom-made god who is more interested in "rights" than righteousness.

Second, America's pulpits are no longer pulpits for delivering God's sacred Word but lecterns for delivering man's quips, quotes, and opinions. This is true for both liberal and evangelical branches of Christendom. The new authority for life and practice is individual experience, and the Ten Commandments have become the "Ten Suggestions."

Third, America's pulpits have become the place of poise for spiritual chameleons seeking to blend with contemporary culture and experience, leading whole congregations of Christian chameleons to blend, without identity, into the warp and woof of a society that so desperately needs the transforming, purifying, cleansing, preserving, and enlightening power and presence of a Holy God walking in the shoes of those who call themselves by His name.

George Gallup, Jr., in *Forecast 2000*, expresses concern that "...only twenty-nine percent (of Americans) feel that organized religion is giving adequate answers to moral problems," and "only thirty-five percent believe that man's spiritual needs are being fulfilled at all by organized religion."[24] Furthermore, "As a people, we lack deep levels of individual spiritual commitment."[25]

How can that be when America still is the most religious nation in the world? It is because our spiritual leaders are not leading. They are, instead, following popular culture and then cloaking it in religious jargon. And we have followed.

The shepherds of God's flock in America must reconsider some things quickly:

- We must consider building men instead of churches.
- We must consider spiritual growth rather than church growth.
- We must consider God's truth over human experience.
- We must consider the awesome consequences for failure to consider all of the above—both before God, and to our society.

If America's churches can't or won't tell the truth, God may have to speak through secular magazines such as *Time*. In the April 5, 1993 issue, the feature article, "The Church Search," warned the pastors of America:

"A growing choir of critics contends that doing whatever it takes to lure fickle customers, churches are at risk of losing their heritage—and their souls."[26]

Mainline churches "are suffering because they have failed to transmit a compelling Christian message to their own children or to anybody else."[27]

A pastor has to shake things up. The point isn't to accommodate self-centeredness but to attack it.[28]

...It is lethal to reshape churches around the claims of returnees who are ignorant of the heritage, or to capitulate to a random set of cravings nurtured by anti-Christian forces.[29]

Biblical truth, "is being edged out by the small and tawdry interest of the self in itself.[30]

Many of those who have rediscovered churchgoing may be shortchanged, however, if the focus of their faith seems subtly to shift from the glorification of God to the gratification of man.[31]

A living, vibrant, Bible-believing, God-obeying church that stands against the tide of popular culture and the exaltation of self is America's only true hope. In America, let our pulpits once again flame with God's righteousness, that we might see truth prevail, and the ills of a suffering society dealt with on God's terms. Perhaps then we will also see a glimmer of America's genius and power reappear on the horizon. For as Abraham Lincoln reminded us, "That nation only is blessed whose God is the Lord."[32]

ANTIDOTE FOR DOOM AND GLOOM

In America's past, when we drifted into spiritual complacency and private and public morals waned, God sent men and women into our midst who carried His truth and delivered it potently so we would hear it and heed it. He delivered it sometimes through unsuspecting sources—once through a baseball player, Billy Sunday, and once even through a lawyer, Charles Finney. Each time, there has been a shaking in America that converted men's minds and turned men's hearts, resulting in restoration of private and public faith and in renewed moral behavior.

There was an "awakening" of mind and spirit which brought renewed life and rigor to the American people. The ultimate consequence was a restoration of national and personal vision and purpose. We—you and I—need such an awakening today. We need to be shaken to our senses so we can once again hear and heed God's message of hope and healing. The true gospel of Jesus Christ is the "good news" antidote for America's present doom and gloom. It is America's only hope. Because it is our only true and lasting hope, I have devoted greater attention to the matter of our faith than to any other issue of life or character. Genuine faith is the glue that binds it all together in integrity. It is what made America unique among nations, and what will revive her once again if we will personally respond and not continue to point our finger at the liberals, the conservatives, the Religious Right, the Religious Left, the government, the preachers, or our parents. "It's me, O Lord, standin' in the need of prayer."

THE PRESENT VALUE OF THE ETERNAL

Many of us have developed progressive myopia—a disease that shortens our visual perception and prevents us from seeing "beyond the end of our nose." We have become trapped by the seeming urgency of life's immediate pressing problems and have become spiritually nearsighted. We struggle frantically to remedy and cope with the cracking world around us or become encased in personal peace and affluence so that we lose sight of the interconnectedness of personal faith and what is going on about us. There is present value in today's world...in downtown or suburban America...to a faith that looks also to eternity.

Once again we look briefly at the findings of secular advertisers, Patterson and Kim, as they now describe the present, tangible value of committed faith in American life:

People describing themselves as 'very religious' definitely make better citizens.[33]

Religious people are more moral than the national average.[34]

Religious people are far less likely to "have a price." [35]

People of faith are "less prone to do something they know is immoral because other people are doing it.[36]

People of faith "are also more at peace with themselves."[37]

Religious people are more likely to say they are satisfied with themselves.[38]

Religious people are...
more truthful,
more committed to family,
make better workers,
less prone to carry weapons, and
less prone to petty crime.[39]

But perhaps more importantly, men and women of strong faith have a sense of direction, of purpose, and of personal worth and value. And it is these intangible needs that Americans are pursuing in every conceivable direction and by every conceivable means...other than where they may truly be found.

WHAT MUST I DO?

A Roman jailer once asked this question. His world was in upheaval and he was under pressure for his very life. A tremendous earthquake had shaken the very foundations of his life, future, and of the jail under his authority. Locked doors flew open, shackles fell off prisoners, and the jailer would pay with his life for a single one who escaped. And as he was about to take his own life in despair, a man of faith—none other than the great apostle Paul—brought a simple message of faith that pierced through the temporal values and pluralistic, everything-goes mindset that bound the jailer in fetters stronger than those of the prisoners he guarded.

And the jailer cried out in the agony of his own empty spirit, "What must I do to be saved?" To which the apostle responded, "Believe on the Lord Jesus Christ, and thou shalt be saved, and thy house."[40] That is what we must do first if we would hear the bells of freedom continue to ring in America. For freedom rings first in the heart of a man or woman before it rings in a nation. And true freedom begins with breaking the shackles of sin that imprison each of us and impress us as slaves to do the bidding of him who presides over evil in our world. Then we will know the truth, and that truth will make us free.

Having set our hearts to pursue the master plan of the God who rules in the affairs of men, let us then...

- Re-establish the Bible, God's Word, as the final authority for our individual lives.

- Choose to exalt and obey the timeless principles of the Bible over the ever-changing dictates of popular culture.

- Teach our children and grandchildren the principles of God's Word with diligence, realizing their future and the future of the nation is at stake.

- Be a living, walking example of God's principles of life, truth, and freedom walking in modern shoes.

- Seek out a church fellowship that is dedicated both in word and practice to teaching the Bible as the authoritative Word of God—unadulterated by popular culture and the new "therapeutic" gospel. If you cannot find such a church, consider starting one with others of like mind and heart.

- Serve your neighbor and fellow Americans, especially those in need, as unto God Himself.

• Do justly, love mercy, and walk humbly with your God.

And America will once again be "One nation, under God." Let freedom ring!

AMERICA'S FINEST HOUR

America's "finest hour" is not the glory of a magnificent military victory but the grace of God being poured out upon us as we fall on our faces in repentance for sin and self-ishness before our true "Founding Father"—God Himself. Then we will see our neighbors differently, our families will be united, crime will diminish, and life will explode with new meaning and purpose as we serve one another under God. This nation will have a new birth of freedom. God will indeed...

> Shed His Grace on Thee
> And crown thy good with brotherhood
> From sea to shining sea.[41]

Will you be the first? Today, if you hear God's voice, Christian or non-Christian, "harden not your heart." TODAY is the day of salvation. There may not be another day for you...or for America. Why do you linger and heed not His mercy? Come home. Home is where the heart is. Turn your heart to the "Founding Father." Turn your heart to Jesus Christ. Become a man or woman of true faith.

And may God, through your example of faith, bless America!

If I would BE served
I must serve.

CHAPTER THIRTEEN

My Brother's Keeper

ON MAY 10, 1773, THE British Tea Act was enacted by Parliament. The Act gave a virtual monopoly for tea distribution to the East India Company, bypassing colonial merchants. Since the American colonies were already chaffing under the tax levied on tea and other goods "without representation," the Tea Act was like rubbing salt into open wounds. The colonists cried out in anguish from the political and economic pain inflicted.

TEA FOR TWO...OR A NATION

On the night of December 16, 1773, the greatest tea party in history unfolded. The cargoes of three tea ships berthed in Boston harbor were unloaded by self-appointed longshoremen disguised as Mohawk Indians. But their contents, rather than being stored in warehouses, were dumped into the harbor, turning the entire harbor into a giant tea cup. And the annals of history preserve the flavor of that event for all of us to taste these two centuries later. It remains a symbol of nonviolent colonial effort to resist British tyranny and oppression. No person or property was destroyed and the colonists even volunteered to pay for the tea, but British retaliation was swift. The Port of Boston was closed and the "Intolerable Acts" were imposed, strengthening and uniting the colonists' resolve. King George declared, "The die is cast. The colonists must either submit or triumph."[1] So a call went out for the Continental Congress to meet in Philadelphia to decide the position of the colonists. Would they submit, or would they triumph?

If there was anyone whose influence had sparked the Boston Tea Party, it was Samuel Adams. He is recorded by history as the "Father of the American Revolution."[2] But Sam Adams was not a wild-eyed revolutionary. He was a man of principle, a man of resolve, commitment, and dedicated service. He was indeed a "public servant" without pay or privilege, and was one of the first voices to be heard in the call to freedom from tyranny.

"The rights of the Colonists as Christians," wrote Adams, "may be best understood by reading and carefully studying the institutes of the great Law Giver...which are to be found clearly written and promulgated in the New Testament."[3] He found not only the seeds of liberty but the call to service set forth in the same Scriptures. And his dedicated service was evident to all. It has been said that up to the time of signing the Declaration of Independence, "No one had done more and perhaps no one else had done so much in behalf of American rights and liberties."[4]

As the tea was being dumped into Boston Harbor, Sam Adams and John Hancock looked on with approval. And it was Adams and Hancock who were promptly labeled by the British as their two most-wanted men.[5] Soon, as Adams and Hancock, under heavy colonial guard, were ushered to safety, Adams remarked in anticipation of the birth of the new nation, "O! what a glorious morning is this!"[6]

From his early forties, Sam Adams made public business his main concern. Although he continued later service in Congress, as governor of Massachusetts and in local offices, his culminating act was the signing of the Declaration of Independence. It was a dream come true after long effort.[7]

Although he was educated at Harvard and acted in positions of prominence, he was no self-seeker. "Unlike John Hancock, he cared nothing for personal glory; to him the cause was paramount, and his most important activities were behind the scenes." He was "notoriously indifferent to his private fortunes."[8]

Perhaps no greater honor can be bestowed upon this patriot of unswerving commitment to serve his fellow man, issuing out of a life dedicated to the God under whose command he served, than the observation of one of his fellow-signers of the Declaration of Independence: "His morals were irreproachable, and even ambition and avarice, the usual vices of politicians, had no place in his breast."[9]

What a heritage to leave to one's children and grandchildren...and to the nation!

HERITAGE OF SERVICE

As Americans, we are blessed with tremendous examples of service. Undoubtedly our first president, George Washington, portrayed the honor of humble service as completely as one could hope to exemplify within the span of three-score and ten years...the years allotted to mortal man. From his early years, he demonstrated leadership in his service. His was not a climb up the social ladder or a self-seeking power grab. Rather, he made himself available to speak, offering his time, his talent, and his treasure to the needs of men and society around him.

After years of interruption of family life to provide both military and political leadership, Washington was ready to retire to the tranquillity of his beloved Mount Vernon. But the needs of a new nation cried for his talents once again. The necessity of the hour prevailed over his longing to withdraw from the arena of public debate to the quiet world of his private retreat overlooking the Potomac. He wanted to run from obligation. How could it be his responsibility? Hadn't he done enough? But he knew the need. Could he leave the fledgling nation at such a time when his countrymen desperately called for his talents? Had not the God who miraculously preserved him in battle under the intensity of enemy fire also bestowed upon him abilities tailored peculiarly to the demands of leading the new government?

He could not walk away. He could not turn his back. And so the general was inaugurated our first president on April 30, 1789. With trembling voice, he called for a Bible, upon which he placed his right hand, taking the oath of office,[10] committing to serve under the divine authority of Him who came in the form of a servant,[11] and taught that "whosoever will be chief among you, let him be your servant."[12] And so the servant was honored, even by his contemporaries as being "First in war, first in peace, first in the hearts of his countrymen."[13]

Washington made a difference among men. But it was not without great personal cost. He did not want to be president, though many wanted to make him king. In a personal letter just thirty days before his inauguration, he revealed his feelings in the starkest reality: "My movements to the chair of Government will be accompanied by feelings not unlike those of a culprit who is going to the place of his execution."[14] In the fall of 1788, without complaining yet revealing his heart about the prospect of being called upon to assume the presidency of these United States, he wrote in another private letter, "If I should conceive myself in a manner constrained to accept, I call Heaven to witness, that this very act [acceptance of the presidency] would be the greatest sacrifice of my personal feelings and wishes that ever I have been called upon to make."[15]

Who can envision the consequences of Washington deciding for the peace and tranquillity of Mount Vernon over shouldering the mantel of responsibility? Many have believed Washington was the key—the essential ingredient—to stabilizing and steering the new nation. Without him, some wondered whether the nation could have survived its birth.[16] You and I, as Americans, are living testimony to the character of the man who said in his heart when torn between self and service, "I am responsible."

SERVANTS OR SLAVES

What will America be tomorrow? Are you responsible? If you and I are not responsible, who is?

It is disconcerting that at this critical hour in the life of our nation, service, responsibility, and commitment have become passé. We now have better things to do—things to better ourselves, things that will help us "get ahead." After all, it's "dog eat dog" in this rough and tumble world. And who is going to fight my battles for me?

This subject of service, commitment, and responsibility has become one of great concern among both secular and religious writers. This is a serious, debilitating problem in American society. It threatens to eat away the very core of civilized society. And it challenges the souls of free men. For we will be either servants or slaves.

176

If we will not choose to serve, neither shall we be served, for ultimately each will serve only himself. When each serves only himself, our masters shall no longer be our "servants" but tyrants...and we shall have become slaves.

Responsibility and commitment are rooted in the character of servanthood. If I choose to serve you, I acknowledge my responsibility and I am committed. If I choose not to serve you, I deny any responsibility to care for you, and I most certainly will avoid any commitment to you.

Most of us love to be served. But, can you imagine a diminishing pool of "servers" and a growing body of "servees"? How long will you consider yourself "served" if the pool of "servers" dwindles to only a few? And how long will the remaining few who serve be able to meet the demand?

At its end, we will no longer appreciate service but *demand* it, seeking to enslave even those few remaining who serve. Gratefulness will gradually disappear and be replaced by thanklessness, requiring either an enslaving master to satisfy my insatiable craving to have my needs met or a violent revolt of the general populace in an effort to compel and coerce the meeting of our needs. Either way, we will have become slaves. We will be either enslaved to an outside tyrant or an internal tyrant...*selfishness*.

THE FREEDOM OF SERVICE

We have met Alexis de Tocqueville earlier in this book. Having spent several years studying American culture after coming to these shores from France in the mid-1800s, he made a shocking observation:

I can see the whole destiny of America contained in the first Puritan who landed on those shores.[17]

This observation requires some further exploration, for in it is embodied perhaps the most profound understanding of what the culture and character of America was all about. From it we can also clearly see our cultural drift and the corrosion of and redefining of character that has occurred in the ensuing years. Our exploration will necessarily be brief.

John Winthrop was a lawyer of considerable means who devoted his life to the welfare of the Puritan colony. Having come to these shores from England while in his early forties, he sought to establish a unique and special kind of society in America...a society built around a strong sense of community. Envisioned was a vibrant, thriving settlement where men and women genuinely cared for one another and sought after the good of others as much as for themselves. It was not to be a commune, but a community. Freedom was to be the driving force...freedom to do what I ought and not just what I want.

And so, before setting foot on the soil that would embrace their venture, the Puritans, under Winthrop's leadership, joined in covenanting together under God to establish "A Model of Christian Charity" in New England. In their own words we witness the simple framework that was to lay the foundation for both law and government in the new land.

> Thus stands the cause between God and us: we are entered into covenant with Him for this work.

> This love among Christians is a real thing, not imaginary....We are a company, professing ourselves fellow members of the body of Christ, [and thus] we ought to account ourselves knit together by this bond of love...[18]

This may sound a bit mushy today. Yet the fragmentation of our society and the growing void in our sense of community and commitment to one another speaks loudly for an injection of the spirit of John Winthrop and those Puritans in this needy hour in America. You see, things were not so wonderful in England as the Puritans set course for America in 1630. They saw the corruption and chaos in society, and yes, even in Christendom. And so historian Perry Miller observes, "Winthrop and his colleagues believed...that their errand was not a mere scouting expedition...it was an essential maneuver is in the drama of Christendom.... It was an organized task force of Christians, executing a flank attack on the corruptions of Christendom."[19]

That is the purpose and call of a new group of Christian believers that the Sovereign Lord of Nations is stirring at this very moment in the great panoply of American history to bring correction, redirection, and new hope and vision to a society run amuck, and to a Christian church that has lost the brilliance of its own light, unable to illumine the way to a society slipping into the abyss. God is calling Christians to be Christians, that His light and His glory may once again be seen in the land.

For Winthrop, that was serious business. At the age of twenty-four, the Cambridge-educated attorney penned these words for his own life:

> I will ever walk humbly before my God, and meekly, mildly, and gently towards all men.... I do resolve first to give myself—my life, my wits, my health, my wealth—to the service of my God and Saviour who, by giving Himself for me and to me, deserves whatsoever I am or can be, to be at His commandment and for His glory.[20]

Thus, American destiny was envisioned by Winthrop in *service*...not in *self*. In their book, *Habits of the Heart*, University of California at Berkeley sociologists led by Robert N. Bellah note, "[Winthrop] decried what he called 'natural liberty' which is freedom to do whatever one wants.... True freedom—what he called 'moral' freedom, 'in reference to the covenant between God and man'—is a liberty 'to that only which is good, just, and honest.' 'This liberty,' he said, 'you are to stand for with the hazard of your lives.' "[21] In commenting on Winthrop's view of life, service, and liberty, these modern-day sociologists from the historic bastions of liberalism, after studying American society today and yesterday, declare:

> His words have remained archetypical for one understanding of what life in America was to be: "We must delight in each other, make other's conditions our own, rejoice together, mourn together, labor and suffer together, always having before our eyes our community as members of the same body."[22]

What is your view? What society do you seek? In what kind of culture do you wish to raise your children? To what philosophy of life do you wish to entrust the future of the America to which your grandchildren will be consigned to live?

Individualism—Blessing or Curse?

We have prided ourselves on our individualism. We parade our models of self-expression on the silver screen before the world. Are we now, as a people, reveling in the sweetness of the fruit of the vineyard we have planted these last generations? Or has the fruit turned sour?

As early as the 1830s, de Tocqueville observed a different strain of freedom and liberty gaining sway in American society from the covenant commitment so beautifully expressed by the Pilgrims and Puritans, whose influence carried the nation for our first two hundred years. He looked at American mores, referring to them as "habits of the heart."[23] And he coined a word, *individualism*, to describe a new idea permeating the culture. He said, "Individualism is a calm and considered feeling which disposes each citizen to isolate himself from the mass of his fellows and withdraw into the circle of family and friends; with this little society formed to his taste, he gladly leaves the greater society to look after itself."[24]

In his book, *Habits of the Heart*, Bellah notes, "Tocqueville saw the isolation to which Americans are prone as ominous for the future of our freedom." And so it is and has become. As a prophet, de Tocqueville described one hundred sixty years ago our present dilemma and the consequences of our shedding the covenant vision of Winthrop and our Pilgrim and Puritan founders. Bellah, in reflecting on de Tocqueville's observations, states, " 'Such folks [individualists] owe no man anything and hardly expect anything from anybody. They form the habit of thinking of themselves in isolation and imagine that their whole destiny is in their hands.' Finally, such people come to 'forget their ancestors,' but also their descendants, as well as isolating themselves from their contemporaries. 'Each man is forever thrown back on himself alone, and there is danger that he may be shut up in the solitude of his own heart.' "[26]

My fellow Americans, our worship at the altar of libertarian individualism has not saved us but enslaved us. We have perverted God's liberty in favor of man's license. Our greatest blessing has become a curse. "Liberty and justice for all" has become liberty and justice for *me*. The chains of our slavery are being forged on the anvil of our selfish hearts. For like Pontius Pilate of old, we ceremoniously wash our hands within the isolation of our minds and say to our neighbor and society, "It's not my responsibility."

The Thomas Jefferson so exalted by hyper-individualists and libertarians feared the scourge of such individualism, concerned that "our rulers will become corrupt, our people careless." "If people forgot themselves 'in the sole faculty of making money,' he said, the future of the republic was bleak and tyranny would not be far away."[27] Jefferson's antidote for such individualism in society was to quote the Scriptures and then extend them to the nation, saying, "Love your neighbor as yourself, and your country more than yourself."[28] So how do we square with that standard?

HOPE FOR A NATION

The problem we face has not changed in six thousand years since the days of Adam and Eve. We merely use different labels today. Adam and Eve had two sons, Cain and Abel. Cain, in the ultimate expression of personal "freedom," murdered his brother in cold blood. When confronted by the voice of God, who holds all men accountable, Cain asked a classic question, "Am I my brother's keeper?"[29] And that question continues to ring down through the annals of time. America's answer to that question is a reflection of her character in this generation; and America's answer is a reflection of your character and mine. Yet the matter goes even deeper, for character is rooted in "habits of the heart."

America's life-and-death struggle for survival is not a battle waged in the halls of political debate or in our courts of law. Neither do the multiplied layers of psychological theories, armchair philosophies, and linguistical gymnastics that seek to re-label, redefine, and camouflage the truth about ourselves bring any meaningful remedy to the problem. Why? Because America has "heart" disease. Our problems are not psychological or sociological...they go to our very heart.

So what speaks to the heart? Doctors perform open-heart surgery on that mass of muscle that pumps life-giving blood throughout our bodies. Arteries are cleaned, replaced, and rerouted. And those who might otherwise find the sentence of death resting upon them receive new life in their mortal bodies. But what do we do with our spiritual "heart"—that which differentiates us as human beings from other living creatures? Can we place psychological Band-Aids over the arterial occlusion of our spiritual life supply and genuinely expect to avoid a massive myocardial infarction in the heart and soul of our nation?

Is there hope in the land to prevent the encroaching gangrene that is deadening America's cities due to lack of life supply? Is rigor mortis inevitable, as many are beginning to believe? Or is there hope for the American heart and the American character? With a resounding voice, I say "THERE IS HOPE!" But we must attend to the "heart" of the matter.

Dr. Tony Evans, a pastor in Dallas, Texas, formed a response to the blight of America's cities called "The Urban Alternative." In his book, *America's Only Hope,* he calls to the Christian church in America to stand up, clean up, and take responsibility as "America's Only Hope."[30] It is interesting that the Frenchman, de Tocqueville, as a "sociologist," also saw the Christian religion as our only hope one hundred sixty years ago.[31] He was not a clergyman, but was an astute observer.

And today, sociologists Bellah and his colleagues from the University of California at Berkeley make a radical turnabout for their profession. Generations of sociologists and psychologists have looked for solutions and explanations for our problems in every nook and cranny of thought, while ridiculing matters of faith. Yet in their much-acclaimed book, *Habits of the Heart,* Bellah and his associates, after five years of study and dialogue, conclude that while our society has been deeply influenced by the traditions of modern individualism, "We have taken the position that our most important task today is the recovery of the insights of the older biblical and Republican traditions."[32]

This may to some seem entirely too theoretical for their blood at this point. But, we are not through with our discussion on our responsibility as citizens amidst a culture war raging violently between the forces of self-centered individualism and those who wish to re-establish a covenant commitment to each other in America. It is the ideas of men that are responsible for the havoc we now witness in this land. And if we refuse at least a cursory exposure to those ideas, we will remain clueless as to our present dilemma—both as to how we arrived at this mess, and as to our only hope for a future that we care to experience.

President Woodrow Wilson spoke to us in an earlier chapter, telling us that a nation that does not know what it "was" does not know what it "is" or where it is going. Sociologist Bellah and associates have traversed, in *Habits of the Heart,* the scope of our history as a nation, and found a resting place in the insightful observations of an independent, outside observer, de Tocqueville. It is in de Tocqueville's comments in *Democracy in America* that both the secret to our amazingly blessed past and our hope for the future rest.

[de] Tocqueville suggested that the economic and political flux and volatility of American society was counterbalanced by the fact that "everything in the moral field is certain and fixed" because "Christianity reigns without obstacles, by universal consent." ...While recognizing that religion "never intervenes directly in the government of American society," he nevertheless considered it "the first of her political institutions." Christianity had the role of placing limits on...individualism, hedging in self-interest with proper concern for others. The "main business of religion," Tocqueville said, "is to purify, control, and restrain that excessive and exclusive taste for well being" so common among Americans.[33]

Well, there is little room for today's concept of religious pluralism in the observations of de Tocqueville. While all are and should be free to practice the "religion" of choice, as a people and as a nation we must make some hard choices as to the foundational principles upon which we wish to build or rebuild a society worth living in. We can practice selfish individualism and experience the temporary "freedom" of every man for himself only so long...and then we pay the awesome price. We are now finding that price too high to pay, and we must return to our roots of righteousness and relationships founded in the Christian faith.

For professing Christians, the task of bringing direction to a society that has enveloped Christendom itself in its headlong pursuit of selfish individualism is indeed challenging. Yet, as Dr. Tony Evans has said, the Christian church is "America's ONLY HOPE!" Yet for so long, he says, "Instead of setting the agenda for society, the church has been crippled by society.... The church is no longer the church in the world; rather, the world is in the church."[34] He continues "Unless the church applies the Bible's truths to every aspect of life, there is little hope for society."[35]

A lawyer came to Jesus Christ to cross-examine Him about

which of the many commandments in Scripture was the greatest. His reply was simple and sets the direction for America today—"Thou shalt love the Lord thy God with all thy heart." This is the first and greatest commandment, He said, and the second is like it, "Thou shalt love thy neighbor as thyself."[36] Another lawyer, John Winthrop, heard those words fifteen centuries later. And it was John Winthrop whose simple yet profound acceptance of the truth of those words formed the basis for the American "Covenant"—an absolute covenant relationship with God out of which we entered a covenant relationship with our fellow citizens. When the two come together again, we will restore the *cross* of Christ in America. We must love God, and we must be our "brother's keeper." That is America's only hope! Will you join me?

As we reach out to serve rather than be served, and to touch the festering wounds of the sons and daughters of America in the name of Christ, the hand of the great Lord of Nations will again begin to move in blessing. The Son of Righteousness will arise in our hearts with healing and forgiveness. And the propitious smiles of heaven will once again grace our land from sea to shining sea.

What can we do to make a difference? What can you and I do to tangibly touch hurting neighbors, fragmented families, greedy government, and a nation rapidly spinning out of control? We will explore some ideas in the next chapter.

To make a DIFFERENCE,
I must MAKE a difference.

CHAPTER FOURTEEN

Compassion That Counts

EVERY WEEK NEW HEADLINES EMBLAZON the pain of a broken society across the front pages of America's newspapers and magazines. Many long to flee from the torrent of destruction to a tranquil place of personal peace...an island of isolation apart from the maddened crowd. Some have, indeed, fled to the hinterlands of forested glades or the acreage of farmlands removed from the incessant contact of people rubbing against each other in aggravation amidst urban life teeming with the pathos of human need.

I have noted the increasing frustration of a people fed up with political platitudes at a time screaming for practical solutions. I, together with most of my countrymen, wince at the crushing burden of a national debt fueled by the "passing of the buck" of social responsibility from ourselves, our families, and churches to the federal government. The cry of the poor and downtrodden causes us to turn our faces as we pass by their pleas scratched on makeshift posters: "Will work for food." A twinge of guilt, or compassion, passes across the membranes of the mind; we feel a sense of helplessness, yet fear that if we should help, someone might take advantage.

I thought the racial issue was under control—until the conflagration of the Los Angeles riots revealed that the coals of racial turmoil had merely smoldered, only to erupt in flames more broadly spread. And now the leaders of America's cities tremble at the tinderbox of social upheaval threatening to explode in violence on Main Street, U.S.A.

Feeling comfortable in my own personal peace and affluence, driving to and from my law office, it was easy to feel relatively insulated from the pain of society, responding only to the needs which passed through my office. It was not that I was living an isolated lifestyle. On the contrary, my law practice placed me in the center of the pushing and shoving of American life in the 1990s. My living has been made in America's favorite combat arena—the courts. Yet somehow, as I drove back and forth to church on Sunday mornings, as a volunteer pastor, and as I spoke in churches and civic clubs throughout California's south land, I found it difficult to bridge the realm of conservative and spiritual principles and the overwhelming needs of society.

In the midst of this cacophony of moral, spiritual, social, and political distress, I attended the National Religious Broadcasting Convention in February 1993. As I worked my way through the numerous exhibits, I turned a corner at the far end of an aisle and stopped short at the massive bronze sculpture in front of me.

Just a year earlier I had been called by a local church to speak on the subject, "The Christian and the Political Issues of the '90s." And I wondered, "What shall I say to people who increasingly despise and distrust politics? Why would God ask me to speak on such a subject when I have not been involved in politics for over fifteen years?" I had asked God to give me a fresh look...and a new heart...to respond to the perplexing issues of our time. The process had begun.

VOICE OF A SCULPTURE

Now, as I stood transfixed by the sculpture before me, I saw modeled in bronze the image of God's living answer to pierce the isolation, brokenness, and hopelessness of a society bereft of meaning, purpose, and direction. It was the image of a "Divine Servant," crafted certainly by divine inspiration in the hands of a Texan, Max Greiner.

I knew then that the future of America would be defined by

a spiritual revival within the heart of America, and especially among the professing Christians of this great land. It would be a revival that would be translated into humble and sacrificial service to a hurting society in the name of Christ. It would take Jesus Himself—well, at least you and I in His name—taking on the form of a servant under His authority. Then, and only then, willing even to "wash one another's feet" as depicted by that sculpture, will the American vision be reborn. Then, and only then, will we experience true reconciliation and restore community. Then, and only then, will *peace* have more than an empty ring and *hope* be more than a four-letter word.

Will you be the first? If not, who will? Let's start on our knees. Now, let's get up and get to work.

WHERE DO I BEGIN?

How can I...how can you...make a difference? What can I do that will count? How can you impact the decaying social, moral, political, and spiritual environment in which you live? What can we do to prevent the tentacles of crime, economic despair, selfishness, moral relativity, racism, illiteracy, malaise, governmental intrusion, and purposelessness from strangling the remaining life out of our families and out of our nation which has brought hope to the world, light in the midst of darkness, healing from the anguish of pain, and freedom, direction, and purpose to past generations?

The most common response to America's dilemma in the last two generations has been an increasing resort either to political power or to governmental programs. Both have significant side effects which are seldom considered in the euphoric pursuit of "quick fixes" that often side-step individual commitment and personal responsibility. Taken alone, resort to political power or governmental programs lead us ever closer to the precipice of social, moral, and cultural collapse. These responses tend to increasingly isolate us from each other. They often create a spirit of antagonism, and they certainly undermine any sense of commitment on a personal level to our neighbor. "Let the government do it," we say. And if we do not say it, we think it. For in our hearts we also think, "How can I, alone, make a difference?"

You *can* make a difference! Yes, even *you* can make a mark to change the direction of American life. You can help stop the moral slide of our culture. You can stave off governmental intrusion into our freedoms. You can preserve justice. You can bring hope where there is despair. You can bring direction and light in a society that is groping in darkness. Say it: "I can make a difference; and with the help of God, I will begin now."

So where do I begin? What are the needs I see around me? Each one of us will undoubtedly have many concerns. But what grabs your heart? What quickens your conscience? Act on it! Do not be paralyzed by fear! "God has not given us the spirit of fear; but of power, and of love, and of a sound mind."[1] Begin with the little things. But begin!

DARE TO CARE

The late psychiatrist Paul Tournier, having endured the horrors of a concentration camp, said, "Happiness is a door opening outward." Unfortunately, we have increasingly closed our minds and hearts to the needs of those around us. Happiness is no longer pursuing us as a nation. Neither are we pursuing true happiness, despite our Declaration of Independence which provides for the "inalienable rights" of "life, liberty, and the pursuit of happiness." Increasingly we seek to isolate ourselves from the needs around us. We determine to protect and insulate our families from the encroaching darkness. And we are becoming so very unhappy. Even our national magazines declare, "The Glooming of America" and other similar themes. There is an antidote for gloom in the midst of social upheaval and cultural crisis. *We must dare to care!*

Consider blooming where you are planted. To begin the thought process:

- Is your neighbor injured or out of work? Take a meal. Talk to your neighbors about assisting. Mow his lawn. Paint her fence.
- Is your mother or father infirm? Take time to talk and care. Coordinate care and concern among the children.
- Assist the teacher in your child's or grandchild's classroom.
- Become involved in the P.T.A. (Parent-Teachers Association).

190

- When a "politically correct" attitude or thought that is morally wrong is presented in private conversation or in a group—speak up with conviction but kindness.

- Take the lead in setting the "agenda" for thought and action in your school, church, and civic club, based on sound and enduring biblical and moral values.

- Take time to teach and model enduring life values for your children and grandchildren. Make it your life "investment." Do not delegate this responsibility to the "professionals."

- Organize or serve in a food bank at your church.

- Dare to organize, or serve in, an AIDS hospice.

- Write sincere and thoughtful letters to your elected representatives...before some massive group effort is amassed.

- Care enough to diligently try to keep current on what is happening around you—in your church, neighborhood, city, state, and nation.

- Discipline yourself. Care enough to pray regularly and with specificity for those in need—for leadership, for national healing, for personal repentance (your own, that is).

- Start, or serve in, a program to encourage literacy.

- Serve the youth in your church, as unto God.

- Open your heart, and your home, in hospitality. It is your heart, not the value of your house, that speaks.

- When you see injustice, speak up, but with respect.

- Visit someone in jail or prison. "Adopt" that person by your thoughtful care.

- Really love your husband or your wife...with deeds of kindness. And then tell him or her regularly...with real words.

- Commit yourself to a local church body. Don't run in from 11:00 to noon on Sunday morning and leave incognito. Be responsible. Don't be a spectator!

- Openly talk among your co-workers, friends, relatives, and neighbors concerning moral and spiritual values. Your silence can be deemed to be agreement with their views.

Be kind and considerate. Do not be argumentative or strident!

- Actively listen! You will be amazed at how it will energize and motivate you to positive response.

- Be *pro*-active, not *re*-active.

- Give liberally of your resources when you see a need. Do *not* defer to the government or think that the "other guy" will do it. That's our problem. If you shouldn't help, why should anyone else?

- Eliminate "they" from your vocabulary. "They" do not usually do anything. Personally identify with the problem and the solution will likely follow—at least your part in the solution.

- Be a better example of moral and ethical behavior than you expect of the "other guy." There is a word for the call to virtue without corresponding practice—hypocrisy!

- Love God—intensely! And let it be reflected in your attitude, care, concern, and commitment to your neighbor. Who is your neighbor? The people, your fellow Americans, and others whom God brings across *your* path...not mine. All of us have "neighbors"—right where we are planted.

Well, that's a start. Bloom where you are planted. God will do the rest.

THE SURROGATE CITIZEN

What happens if I do not "bloom where I am planted?" What can we expect if we reject service to others and sacrifice? What if we decline to shoulder moral responsibility?

A "surrogate" is something that replaces the real thing. If a parent refuses to "parent," the court will appoint a relative or even a stranger to substitute for the parent. What happens when you or I abdicate our care and responsibilities as citizens? What are the consequences when I demand my rights and shirk my duties? The "surrogate citizen"—the government—steps in to assume responsibility. In America, we euphemistically refer to this surrogate citizen as "Uncle Sam."

A surrogate never quite replaces the real thing. Something is lost, in spirit if not in substance. We despise and kick up our heels at government intrusion on our liberties, yet more often than not we bring it upon ourselves. It is said, "The death of democracy is not likely to be an assassination from ambush. It will be a slow extinction from apathy, indifference, and under-nourishment."[2] Alexis de Tocqueville observed, "The health of a democratic society may be measured by the quality of the functions performed by private citizens."[3]

Consider again for a brief moment:

- Governmental involvement in "Social Security" resulted from children, families, and churches increasingly failing to care for their own.

- Governmental insistence upon national health care resulted from children, families, and churches increasingly failing to care for their own—fueled by growing greed in the entire health care field that priced care out of reach, bringing on governmental intervention.

- Companies failed to govern the quality and safety standards of products, resulting in government regulation.

- Companies failed to reasonably respond to environmental concerns, bringing on the heavy hand of government to overregulate.

- Parents increasingly abused or failed to supervise their children, resulting in the courts and government responding to excess, interfering even with legitimate parenting under the guise of the "states for the child's 'best interests.'"

Once the "surrogate citizen" intervenes, it is nearly axiomatic that the particular area of intervention is forever forfeited by the citizens. The wattage of "freedom's holy light" is reduced—until there is no longer a flicker. But loving service and compassionate caring keeps the flame of freedom burning. What causes your spirit to come alive, another government program to meet needs, or the sacrificial caring of your "neighbor"?

The signpost of another government "takeover" has just been planted. Service and financial provision by individuals, families, churches, and other organizations have so waned that *national* "service" is now being proposed by our president for our youth, so as to pay for or compensate for educational "loans."[4] On the surface this may appear noble...but *next it will be national* service for adults for various and sundry reasons. In a March 22, 1993 editorial on the subject, *Newsweek* states, "The nation is coming apart at the seams and people don't connect with one another anymore." If we will not serve one another, we will serve the "surrogate citizen."

COMPASSION THAT COUNTS

Compassion is not a "feeling" but an "act." In reading the New Testament, there are numerous instances where it is recorded that Jesus Christ "took compassion." In each instance, he did something tangible to respond to the need. It was an essential ingredient to "fleshing out" the gospel of salvation. It was "good news," both for the spirit and the body.

Believe it or not, this was also an essential ingredient of the American vision which John Winthrop, the lawyer we spoke of in earlier chapters, sought to introduce on these shores in the 1600s. It was part of the American covenant—a covenant to love God expressed tangibly in a covenant to touch our neighbor with God's love through human hands. Winthrop spent his own small fortune to instill the reality of that covenant in the fabric of our society in the Puritan colony. And for that reason he could confidently say, "...we shall be as a City upon a Hill..."[5] Our American "city" is sliding off that "hill" because our spiritual foundations are undermined and decayed, but some of our fellow citizens are working to make a difference.

Crisis Pregnancy Center

A young Christian lawyer in Pasadena, California, was grieved over the massive blight on the nation brought on by abortion. He felt it was not sufficient to voice objections to abortion. Real help was needed. So he helped develop and launch a crisis pregnancy center to counsel and assist troubled young mothers-to-be, affording them alternatives, in order to spare the lives of their unborn babies.[6]

Racial Reconciliation

A white executive of perhaps the largest Christian mission organization in the world intentionally moved his family to riot-torn South-Central Los Angeles to be a "human bridge" of reconciliation between white and black Americans.[7]

Uplifting AIDS Sufferers

An evangelical Christian minister became burdened for one of the great tragedies of American society—those people suffering from AIDS. He began giving his time in AIDS hospices to bring encouragement and companionship. His heart has expanded to create "Project Compassion," which coordinates the efforts of many churches, not only to help those suffering from AIDS, but to provide housing for the homeless, crisis pregnancy assistance, job placement, and clothing and food for those in need.[8]

Community Development

A black Mississippi minister, unmercifully beaten by white Americans, forgave those who persecuted him. Having been freed from the bondage of bitterness and hatred, he intentionally moved his family into one of the most dangerous, drug-infested communities in southern California to provide hope, education, and new vision for kids. He now shares his concepts for reconciliation and redevelopment of America's inner cities around the nation.[9]

Literacy/Public Policy

A young, black Christian lawyer, concerned about the devastating consequences of illiteracy among youth near her Pennsylvania home, developed a literacy program involving 400 children. This same female lawyer was grieved over the affect of governmental policies undermining the family, so she established a public-interest law firm to speak to policy issues affecting the basic building block of our society.[10]

Prison Ministry

A powerful lawyer in the White House, having himself been convicted and imprisoned, was dramatically converted to faith in Jesus Christ. He translated his new love for God into practical "touching" of the lives of other prisoners—giving them new hope through reconciliation with God. Prison Fellowship has now spread through prisons across America and throughout the world.[11]

Love, Inc.

An ordinary American saw the need to match the love and resources of people in churches across the nation with a wide range of human need. Now, church people who are concerned about the needy, the hungry, and the homeless are networked with the needy in their neighborhoods. The chronically dependent are being helped to become independent, delivering them from the bondage of welfare.[12]

You and a Needy Nation

Are you ready to "take" compassion? Can you see the need around you? Are you ready to "speak" with your time, talent, and treasure to the hopelessness and pain of those around you whose cry causes heaven to weep? Is your heart broken with those things that break the heart of God? Where do you fit? Let's break the "culture of complaint," our "victim" mentality, and our dependence on the "surrogate citizen" by reaching out with compassion that counts. Make a difference...TODAY!

Christian, let's act with compassion in the name of Christ. Add one hundred pounds of integrity to your message. American, if you do not act in the name of Christ, under whose authority do you act? There are only two ultimate spiritual authorities. Lincoln declared in his Gettysburg Address, "This nation, under God, shall have a new birth of freedom, that government of the people, by the people, for the people shall not perish from the earth." Let's serve under God's authority. Let's *PRESERVE US A NATION!*

196

If I would be self-governed,
I must SELF-govern.

CHAPTER FIFTEEN

A Civil Body Politic

ON NOVEMBER 21, 1620, FORTY-THREE
Pilgrims were about to set foot on American soil for the first
time. They were concerned that the nature and purpose of their
endeavor, which had been taken at great risk and had already
cost many their lives, be clearly expressed to preserve the
future of their intentions. And so they penned a short document
to memorialize their intentions. That document, known as the
"Mayflower Compact," was the first document setting forth the
meaning of "America," and set the tone for the nation that
would grow and prosper under that vision. It stated:

> Having undertaken for the Glory of God, and
> Advancement of the Christian Faith, and the Honor of our
> King and Country, a voyage to plant the first colony in
> the northern Parts of Virginia; do by these Presents,
> solemnly and mutually in the Presence of God and one
> another, covenant and combine ourselves together into a
> civil Body Politick, for our better Ordering and
> Preservation, and Furtherance of the Ends aforesaid;[1]

All that would fulfill their goal of "Advancement of the
Christian Faith" for God's glory in establishing the new nation
was to be accomplished by "a civil Body Politick" which would
be created as they would "combine ourselves together...for our

199

better Ordering and Preservation." Thus was instituted for the first time in history a government of "we the people."

If our government is "we the people," logic and reason dictate that without "we the people," we have no government. Therefore, government in America requires you and me. We are all part of the "Civil Body Politick." We cannot escape it. That is what is meant by "self-government."

American government is not a "they," it is a "we." In a sense, government for us is a non-delegable duty, except that we do elect representatives. When we elect representatives, we elect people like ourselves whom we collectively believe represent who we are, what we believe, our goals, our aspirations. For that reason it has been said "we get the government we deserve."

If I am an American, I am involved in politics, for I am part of the "Civil Body Politick" in a self-governing nation. If I am not involved in "politics," I am not part of the "Civil Body Politick" and must question whether I am an American. Politics is therefore the means whereby we work out our relationships with one another in covenant commitment. It does not mean I must run for office. It does mean, however, that in some way we are all necessarily "politicians" because we must all work out our relationships with one another under the umbrella of our covenant "for better Ordering and Preservation and Furtherance of the Ends" for which the nation was established.

Viva La Difference!

What difference does it make? Why must we grind into our consciousness that we are self-governed? We must because it is that which set America uniquely apart from all previous governments in the history of civilization. It is what makes us what we are. It is the foundation of all that made America great. And it is the basis on which we became "one nation under God." For "we the people" voluntarily chose, in establishing the nation, that we would submit to God's authority. We established the nation, "for the Glory of God, and Advancement of the Christian Faith."[2] This theme, from the Pilgrims, was repeated by the Puritans. And Puritanism, believe it or not, "laid the egg of democracy."[3]

The concept of freedom and liberty enjoyed by Americans

was born out of religious freedom. The Pilgrims and Puritans were convinced true freedom and liberty for all would continue only to the extent the colonists submitted to the authority of God and His will as expressed in the Bible. The people had to repeatedly choose...and re-choose to submit to God's authority. They found a critical link between their prosperity as a "Civil Body Politick" and their intentional choice to submit to God's authority in their individual and corporate lives.[4]

That theme continued for a century-and-a-half, to the time of the American Revolution. Even Benjamin Franklin, not particularly known for his faith, declared publicly in the Constitutional Convention when addressing George Washington as chairman, "I have lived, Sir, a long time, and the longer I live, the more convincing proofs I see of this truth—that God governs in the affairs of men." Franklin went on to say, "We have been assured, Sir, in the Sacred Writings, that except the Lord build the house, they labor in vain that build it."[5]

Who is building the American "house" today? Who is maintaining it? "We the people" have a choice. The "house" of our "Civil Body Politick" must be continually maintained. If it is maintained, it is maintained by "we the people." If we do not maintain it, the house begins to deteriorate and crumble. Look around you. Does the fracturing of our society indicate anything about the condition of the "house" of our "Civil Body Politick"? Have our mortal minds and consciences become so seared that we cannot assimilate the meaning of the statistics we ourselves publish?

Self-government means we must govern our *selves*. If we fail to govern ourselves, we are not *self*-governed. Our ability to govern ourselves has historically proven to be in direct proportion to our willingness, both individually and corporately, to submit to the governance and authority of God.

This is not "religious" talk. This is real life stuff! How long can we who pride ourselves as the most scientifically advanced nation in the world continue to ignore the cause-and-effect relationship between our national sickness and our national sin? Can we afford to continue "playing pretend" in our individual lives, in our families, and as a nation?

America's number one crisis is not the economy—and it's

not crime, health care, violence, AIDS, divorce, or any of the other numerous problems that threaten to overwhelm us. America's number one crisis is an "authority" crisis! And "we the people," as self-governors, must make a choice. Will we return to being "one nation under God"? Or will we arrogate ourselves to the throne of our lives and declare ourselves "god"?

If our Declaration of Independence is to have further value to us, we must, both individually and as a people, declare our "dependence" upon the "Power that hath made and preserved us a nation."[6] Power politics and political platitudes are utterly ineffectual in the face of our national crisis. Have we not realized that yet? Or are we still building our hopes on the sand of eternal optimism that things will just get better? As we wait, our nation is crumbling. We do not need a new paint job; we need reconstruction from the inside out.

We must humble ourselves, pray, seek the face of God Himself and His forgiveness, and repent.[7] This is true for all of us including all brands of the Christian Church in America. For the very Scriptures we purport to believe declare, "...judgment must begin at the house of God."[8]

A CHOICE FOR THE PEOPLE

We have a choice! It is a "life or death" choice. Time is too late to mince words. Our first president warned us in his farewell address, "Reason and experience both forbid us to expect that National morality can prevail in exclusion of religious principle."[9] John Adams, our second president, warned us again, "Our Constitution was made only for a moral and religious people. It is wholly inadequate to the government of any other.... We have no government armed with power capable of contending with human passions unbridled by morality and religion."[10]

Moses similarly warned the nation of Israel, after delivering God's laws and authority to them, saying, "I have set before you life and death, blessing and cursing..." Then he gave them a "subtle" hint for their self-governing choice—"Choose life," he said, "that both thou and thy seed may live...and that thou mayest dwell in the land...."[11] Israel's history is a cyclical history of blessing when they chose to honor God's authority and of cursing when they chose to come out from under that authority.

Abraham Lincoln, our sixteenth president, pointedly declared the source of America's blessing: "It is the duty of nations, as well as of men, to own their dependence upon the overruling power of God and to recognize the sublime truth announced in the Holy Scriptures and proven by all history, that those nations only are blessed whose God is the Lord."[12]

America stands at the crossroads of history. So do you...and your family. As Joshua of old cried out to ancient Israel, so I cry out to you, my fellow American, "Choose you this day whom ye will serve...but as for me and my house, we will serve the Lord."[13]

BE INVOLVED

Having made our fundamental choices, we must be involved in the fray. If we will be self-governed, we must govern ourselves. That means we must be informed and be involved. It is our "civic duty" arising out of our covenant to one another as a "Civil Body Politick." But the goal is to serve, not to coerce or to "lord it over" our fellow citizens. Public service means public service. Our attitude is as important as our position.

LABELS ARE LIBELS

Have we lost our ability to speak with clear and convincing speech? "Political correctness" has gained a stranglehold on our ability to communicate in good faith with one another. That is a violation of our covenant. We cannot "mutually covenant and combine ourselves" "for our better Ordering and Preservation" when we create artificial barriers in the common language which prevent any sense or hope of mutuality.

Our labels become "libels" when they preempt discussion. As a "Civil Body Politick," let us strive openly and in good faith in the "public square," in open forums. Resist the temptation to conform to political correctness. It is an adult form of peer pressure. It is insincere. And it is calculated to squeeze you into the labeler's mold. It is designed to remove critical subjects from both public and private discourse. Avoid it like the plague!

A BLOW TO THE LEFT—A BLOW TO THE RIGHT

To the Left

To my fellow Americans on the "left" or "liberal" end of the political spectrum—do you really, in the name of "compassion," want to continue the expansion of government control and involvement in our private lives that squeezes out the lifeblood of the very freedom and liberty you purport to champion?

On the other hand, in the name of "liberty," do you really want the tyranny of social anarchy in exchange for the formal and systematic removal of "the God Who gave us liberty" from the schools for our young and the halls of public debate? For if my history is correct, virtually every significant social reform in American history that you now tout so highly was spearheaded or encouraged by strong, Bible-believing Christians in the name of Christ.

And was it not your standard-bearer, Thomas Jefferson, who declared, "Indeed I tremble for my country when I reflect that God is just, that His justice cannot sleep forever"?[14] And was it not that same Jefferson who penned the words in the great Declaration of Independence declaring it to be a "self-evident truth" that all of the rights of liberty which you purport to espouse were "endowed by their Creator"? Does that document of liberty not conclude with "a firm reliance on the protection of Divine Providence" and commence with an acknowledgment that "the laws of nature and of nature's God" entitle men to a station of authority to be independent?[15]

Perhaps there should be some intellectual integrity in acknowledging Mr. Jefferson's letter to the Danbury Baptists in 1803, calling for a "wall of separation" to keep the government out of the church rather than keeping the church out of government. Perhaps ground would also be gained in restoring the nation by acknowledging that interpretation as being the clear understanding of the courts of the land for 150 years until an increasingly "liberal" Supreme Court decided to ignore legal precedent, set aside the rules of judicial interpretation under *stare decisis,* and excise the words *wall of separation* from the context of Jefferson's letter, thus redefining an otherwise clearly understood doctrine to suit a liberal notion.[16] Have you not undermined the very divine Authority that made and "preserved us a nation," as declared in our National Anthem?

Such mental, legal, and historical gymnastics present insurmountable hurdles for "conservatives" and appear to be nothing short of intellectual dishonesty under the cloak of law. Are not the very foundations of the Republic at risk when individual rights are radically promoted without corresponding responsibility, while at the same time God's authority to speak in our individual and corporate life is mocked and repudiated and is locked out of the halls of public debate?

To my fellow Americans on the "right" or "conservative" end of the political spectrum, where I admit I generally can be found—could we not more effectively articulate what we are "for" as compared to what we are "against"? Have we not unnecessarily alienated some by giving the perception that people are secondary to economics?

And specifically to the so-called "Christian Right," from the confessions of one of our standard bearers, have we not failed to formulate an "overarching, universal theme which could be articulated about where [we] wanted to take America?...Because of this lack of unifying message, the movement created misunderstanding, resentment, and even fear among potential allies."[17]

Did we not lack "visible compassion"? And by that lack, did we not "forfeit the trust of the populous and abdicate the right to lead the nation"? In our "self-proclaimed quest for national righteousness...[didn't] the Christian Right overlook God's equally important imperatives for justice and mercy for the oppressed, the poor, the less fortunate, and for our neighbors?"[18]

Is it not true that "because our message was not perceived as being firmly rooted in a foundation of love and compassion, we lacked the moral authority to command loyalty and we lacked the vision to attract zeal, energy, and sacrifice"?[19] Was not "the failure of the Christian Right to follow Christ in serving our community the major obstacle to accomplishing its national objective"?[20]

RACISM, RHETORIC, AND RECONCILIATION

Racism is a reality! It has no place in our "Civil Body Politick" and is repugnant to our covenant with God and our fellow man. "We the people" must, with God's help, eradicate this blight from our hearts and society.

But fundamentally, racism is not a problem that can be remedied by legislation. It can be accomplished only by "heart surgery." There is only one qualified for such surgery and that is the "Great Physician." "Liberal" demands, confrontation, and stridency serve no ultimate purpose and only provide excuse to drive the roots of racism deeper. On the other hand, "conservative" games of "pretend" that racism is neither real nor rampant only exacerbate the frenzy of strident activists.

So where does that leave us? Black America, our preeminent "minority" at present, has a unique place in our history. There is a spirit that overshadows the nation with roots deeply entwined in the fabric of our society and culture. Racism has become a two-way street, if not a multi-hubbed intersection. It defies solution by coercion or ingenuity. It is a matter of the heart. And "habits of the heart" must be dealt with in the realm of our faith under the authority of God Himself. There is that "authority" problem again.

The first two great spiritual awakenings in our nation resulted in massive social impact and in the cleansing of many social evils. Slavery was confronted by revivalists in each. George Whitefield was a champion against slavery before the Revolutionary War. Charles Finney cried out in opposition to slavery before the Civil War. And we are long overdue for another spiritual revival in our "Civil Body Politick" in America.

I and many observers are convinced America faces her greatest crisis ever in this precipitous moment of her history. A mournful cry issues from saint and sinner alike amidst the agony of the tearing of the flesh and fabric of our society. Prayer goes up from churches across the land as Christians plea for revival as America's only hope. Yet the "Lord's hand is not shortened, that it cannot save; neither his ear heavy, that it cannot hear."[21] I am convinced the God who gave us liberty will no longer tolerate a church that in both black and white congregations not only tolerates but perpetuates America's "national sin" of racism. Our iniquity has not only separated us from each other but "your iniquities have separated between you and your God. . . that he will not hear."[22]

The time has come for judgment to begin at the house of God in our "Civil Body Politick." We are praying for revival with "unclean hands." God has not "winked" at our failure to cleanse this stain of racism from His church in America in two previous "awakenings." I am convinced the reconciliation of black and white believers in American Christendom is a co-extensive condition, if not a pre-condition, to the great move of God's hand and spirit so desperately sought and so drastically needed across the face of these United States.

The Supreme Ruler of Nations desires to strip out the Mason-Dixon Line from His church in America. He will not tolerate a church with spot or wrinkle...or any such thing.[23] And here's further food for thought: I recall reading in the Sacred Writings that God did not send His Spirit in power until His people were "in one accord."[24]

CHOICES

It is twilight on the American horizon. Unless there is divine intervention, history will record the "rise and fall" of another empire. But the choice is ours. Will we—both you and I—submit to God's authority? Or will we continue the cry of our age, "I'll do it my way"? The jury is out deliberating, but the verdict is not yet in. There is time to settle this issue. But what we do, we must do quickly. And this is a decision we must make both individually and in corporate consensus.

Alexis de Tocqueville noted a century ago, "Not until I went into the churches of America and heard her pulpits flame with righteousness did I understand the secret of her genius and power."[25] Let our pulpits again flame, not with rhetoric, but in righteousness. And may that flame kindle in each of our hearts, that the blaze of a Holy God's light and glory may sweep across our land and PRESERVE US A NATION!

CHAPTER SIXTEEN

The Integrity Gap

ON JUNE 14, 1777, THE Second Continental
Congress adopted this resolution:

"Resolved that the flag of the United States be thirteen stars,
white in a blue field, representing a new constellation."[1]

Whether or not history can verify the accepted creator of the
first flag as Betsy Ross, history can confirm the blessing those
Stars and Stripes have brought to Americans, and even to the
world.

I can never remember a time—even as a young boy—when
my heart did not skip a beat when I spotted Old Glory waving
in the breeze. Perhaps this is because my birthday happens to
be Flag Day. After all, not everyone is so privileged as to have
an entire nation put out its flags on one's birthday. But I know
other Americans have shared and felt the bond, the unity, and
the sense of pride and purpose that our flag represents in our
hearts.

AN ALLEGIANCE GAP

But a flag is a symbol, not the substance. And when the substance it represents changes, dissolves, or is distorted, the symbol also begins losing its meaning. When the nation loses its
integrity, the flag loses its bond of allegiance, and when the flag

209

no longer holds respect among the people, there is clear evidence of severe internal decay. Such is our current plight in this great land we hold dear. We are developing an "allegiance gap" because we have an "integrity gap."

In 1892, our Pledge of Allegiance was written by Francis Bellamy and was published in the magazine, *Youth's Companion*.[2] Millions of Americans since have proudly stood in public gatherings and saluted the Stars and Stripes. As we respectfully placed our hands over our hearts, declaring those familiar words, "I pledge allegiance to the flag of the United States of America..." we shared an understanding. It was a mutual conviction that America was good, that America stood for justice, truth, virtue, and honor, which led us to continue our pledge, "...and to the Republic for which it stands."

And now we are beginning to ask ourselves, "What do we stand for today?"

What do we stand for? If we don't stand for something, we'll fall for anything.

Our children once saluted the flag daily in schoolrooms across America. Today, well, some do, some don't. It's "ho-hum, take it or leave it." There is little sense today of national purpose, direction, or virtue. Quietly, we wonder why. And then most of us just shrug our shoulders and go off to business as usual. We bellyache about the waning "American Dream." But what has happened to the American spirit? How have we lost our allegiance?

We need not look far to answer the question. It is not a mystery. For as I said, the allegiance gap is, at its root, an integrity gap. We began questioning our leadership during the Vietnam War. Then came Watergate and, later, "Iran-gate." These were followed by "Rubbergate"—the check-bouncing scandal in which members of Congress intentionally overdrew their accounts in the House Bank.[3] That brought us to the 1992 presidential election (which I'll call "Character-gate"), when America decided that personal integrity was a value well worth sacrificing for the promise of temporary economic relief.[4] Now we are trudging our way through "Moral-gate" into a world where moral principles that have guided and protected us for centuries are given short shrift and are cast away as unwanted refuse in the face of a cry for individual "rights" and selfish, "politically correct" pursuits.

It is no wonder we don't like what we see in our national mirror. How can I, you, or we pledge allegiance to a nation that is losing its integrity? Will Rogers, an inveterate optimist who said he never met a man he didn't like, made an interesting observation in his autobiography back in 1949. He said, "If we ever pass out as a great nation, we ought to put on our tombstone, 'America died of the delusion she had moral leadership.' "[5] In other words, moral leadership is the key to the greatness and even the survival of our nation. President Eisenhower, in his first inaugural address in 1953, reflected, "Whatever America hopes to bring to pass in the world must first come to pass in the heart of America."[6]

What is in the heart of America today? What is in your heart? America is not a feeling or a political whim or a patriotic euphoria. America is "we the people." And for America to change, we the people must change. We cannot expect the president or Congress to change unless we are willing to change. A recent editorial in *Time* magazine states, "As voters we profess shock that our candidates should behave as we do. The paradox is striking. Voters are demanding in their leaders the personal virtues that they decreasingly demand of themselves. There is a word for the profession of virtue accompanied by practice of vice—hypocrisy."[7] And so we the people widen the allegiance gap, unwilling to clean up the image we see in the national mirror. As goes our integrity, so goes our allegiance.

THE INTEGRITY GAP

The U.S. Supreme Court was asked some years ago to define "pornography." The oft-quoted response of one of the justices was, "I'll know it when I see it." Similarly, most of us have some ill-defined conception of what "integrity" should look like. We believe we will know it when we see it. That means that integrity is something we believe we can observe. Yet integrity is not an object. It is not something we can reach out and touch. But we know in our hearts it is real when it is present...and a very real need exists when it is absent.

The trouble in America today, however, is that with the erosion of moral absolutes, the lines of integrity have become blurred. If every man is allowed the "freedom" to define his own morals, doesn't every man have the right to define his own integrity? Without a moral consensus among "we the people," we forfeit the right to a common expectation of standard integrity.

Thus, a thief who is consistent in his thieving, stealing from the "right" people for the "right" purpose, is an "honorable" thief under the then-prevailing "moral" expectations or "politically correct" motivations of the general society. It should not take a theologian or rocket scientist to comprehend where the denial of moral absolutes is leading us. For we are making it increasingly difficult to identify integrity "when we see it." We have an "integrity gap."

George Barna, in his recent report on the results of polling Americans on our beliefs, values, and direction, entitled his book-length report *Absolute Confusion*.[8] He is only one of a rising chorus of voices to make this assessment. But I am convinced there is yet hope if we will, as individuals, seriously explore our personal and individual role and responsibility— both in how we contributed to our present confusion, and in how we will respond to restore life-giving, hope-inspiring integrity to a decaying culture. It is clear that if we sincerely wish to bridge the "integrity gap," we need to get a better grip on the meaning of integrity.

WHAT IS INTEGRITY, ANYWAY?

Although we believe in our hearts we will know integrity when we see it, most of us find it easier to identify integrity— or its absence—in the "other guy," rather than in ourselves. If there is to be any real bridging of the integrity gap in America, it must begin with me, and with you.

Are you a man or woman of integrity? What does your wife think? Or your husband? What would be the private report of your business associates, your co-workers, or your neighbors? Has your life served to be a living definition of integrity for your children or your grandchildren? Has your behavior, your individual acts from day to day, reflected your professed values? It's time to "get real" about these things! This is the "stuff" of integrity.

The word *integrity* is related to the word *integer*, which basically means "whole." Does your life "come together" in a visible, identifiable "whole"? Do my individual acts, words, attitudes, and thoughts line up consistently with some standard I value? If so, what is that standard? Can you define your life standard for your children? Is your life a living testimony of that standard to those around you?

Don't try to get off the hook by saying, "Well, nobody is perfect!" We all know that. The time for excuses is long past. The question is, "Does my behavior and my life demonstrate a consistent, observable course in the direction of my professed values?" Or perhaps we could ask, "Do I meet the standard for integrity that I hold for others—my boss, my spouse, my congressman, my pastor or priest?" Let's briefly explore the recesses of our lives together. Here are some questions that can begin the process. I am sure you can add a few others of your own. Are you ready? I wince as I begin, for I know a few of my own imperfections. But let's get on with it. Let's each ponder "the shoe that fits" and begin to do something about it.

A PROBE FOR INTEGRITY

Raise your right hand. Do you solemnly swear the testimony you are about to give shall be the truth, the whole truth, and nothing but the truth? Please state and spell your name for the record.

The last time you received too much change by the cashier, did you return the excess?

The last time you were undercharged by the waiter, cashier, or salesperson, did you voluntarily offer to pay the additional amount due?

Did you do anything recently that would grieve you or make you angry if you knew your spouse had done the same thing?

Did you this last year call in sick to your employer and then go off and do personal pleasure or business?

Have you permanently "borrowed" your employer's supplies (pencils, pens, etc.)?

Have you delayed paying a bill when you could have made timely payment by adjusting your personal desires?

(NOTE: This is the "stuff" that tears up America's integrity quotient. Shall we go on?)

Have you told your secretary to say, "I'm not in" or your child to say, "I'm not home," when you really were?

Did you report *all* of your cash income last year on your tax return?

Did you write an "illness" note to your child's teacher when you really took the child out of school for some fun family activity?

Do you complain about the violence and sex excesses of television or the movies and then watch them anyway, or rent a video so you can watch it in your home where no one will see you?

Did you take care of personal affairs on your boss's time and report it as "work" time?

Do you make personal long-distance calls from work so you don't have to pay for them on your tab at home?

(Time out: The list could be endless. I think it's necessary, however, to touch my Christian brothers and sisters a little in some important areas.)

Do you say you believe the Bible as God's divinely inspired, authoritative Word? If so:

- Have you used the Lord's name loosely? Ponder this awhile. Some have developed a habit.
- Do you tithe to the church?
- Do you read your Bible daily?
- Do you give to the poor or seek out the needy?
- Did you divorce your spouse even though he or she had not committed adultery?
- Have you cheated on your spouse?
- If your children were a jury, would they convict you of being a godly example?

(Time for a breather! The list may not be exhaustive, but it sure is exhausting, isn't it? It's time now for the leaders of Christian ministries. Are you ready?)

- Do you raise money under false pretenses?

- Do you pay all of your ministry bills? On time?
- Do you attempt to manipulate people?

Publishers:

- Will you publish almost anything if you think it will make a big profit?
- Will you make deals with celebrities to have books published under their name to increase the profit margin when they didn't write the book?

Pastors:

- Are you so hungry to lure people to your church that you would modify, compromise, or just not talk about the straight truth of God's Word, as it would impinge upon the rough-and-tumble areas of people's lives?
- Do you preach "the whole counsel of God" even if it is uncomfortable, or you feel you may risk your position, or you believe it may not be "politically correct"?

Have we gone beyond such "trivia"? It is this "trivia" that has burned a hole in the soul of America. Is this chapter for any of us...or is it just for the "other guy"?

THE DEATH OF ETHICS

Ethics are closely related to, and are a significant component of, integrity. While American professionals run to and fro from one ethics course to another, true ethics lie gasping on their deathbed in the "land of virtue."

"The number one cause of our business decline is low ethics by executives. Who says so? Workers and the executives themselves."[9]

Syndicated columnist Cal Thomas, in his book, *The Death of Ethics in America,* notes, "The lack of any personal accountability to a moral code has made immorality respectable in our nation."[10] He calls this "An American Tragedy."[11]

Richard C. Halverson, chaplain of the U.S. Senate, made this observation:

"Abandoning an absolute ethical/moral standard leads irresistibly to the absence of ethics and morality. Each person determines his own ethical/moral code. That's

215

anarchy. Evil becomes good—good becomes evil. Upside down morality! Good is ridiculed! Evil is dignified!"[12]

A candidate for political office was interviewed on television by a news reporter. When asked about ethics and character issues in his personal life, he angrily retorted, "That's none of your business! What I do on my own time doesn't make a bit of difference as far as my candidacy for political office is concerned."[13] Is this true? Do you believe it? Such was not always the case in these United States.

A discussion of ethics and integrity would be seriously deficient without a reminder from the life of our sixteenth president, Abraham Lincoln. His life was replete with examples of honor, ethics, and integrity—yes, even as a lawyer. Justice Sidney Breese of the Supreme Court remarked that Lincoln was "the fairest lawyer I ever knew."[14]

But two examples stand out to test the mettle of our own ethical standards. When he was a shopkeeper, Lincoln, having discovered on one occasion that he had taken six-and-one-quarter cents too much from a customer, walked three miles that evening after the store closed to return the money.[15] On another occasion, he weighed out a half-pound of tea, or he believed he had. It was the last thing he had done before closing up that night.

On returning the next morning, he discovered a four-ounce weight on the scales. He immediately closed the shop and hurried to deliver the remainder of the tea. His care in his personal ethics earned him the title "Honest Abe."[16] And it was this integrity that enabled him to lead the nation through its darkest and most difficult hour of that day. What will enable you and me to lead our nation in this dark hour at the close of the twentieth century? Are we qualified? We can and must act promptly in our own lives. Lincoln practiced what he preached. America is waiting for a repeat performance from you...and from me.

SPEAKING OF PREACHING

If I would practice what I preach, it becomes important what I preach. So what do you preach? Our lives are an open book. Our children, grandchildren, neighbors, and co-workers cannot hear the good things we say for seeing the contradictory things we do, consistently. Our behavior "preaches" loudly, whether we like it or not. And while character is made by many acts, it may be lost by a single act. And the collapse of character often begins on compromise corner.

While our behavior preaches loudly, it is nevertheless critical what we say. So then, what have we been saying about integrity? We can answer that question only by looking behind the desired integrity to the components that, together, comprise the label of "integrity." Those are qualities of character and moral behavior. So what have we been saying about moral behavior? Precious little!

FROM THE SECULAR SIDE

An insightful article in *Forbes* magazine gives a "message to society: What you applaud, you encourage. And: Watch out what you celebrate."[17] What do we celebrate, applaud, and encourage generally as a society? We need only take a look at the entertainment we pipe into our homes and pump through the delicate membranes of our minds and hearts.

Michael Medved, co-host of the weekly PBS television program "Sneak Previews," in a recent address to hundreds of college students, declared, "The Hollywood dream factory has become a poison factory." As a film critic recognized in the industry, he states, "The crisis of popular culture is at its very core a crisis of values." He then observes, "No movie is morally neutral, no movie fails to send a message, no movie doesn't change you to some extent when you see it. Movies have a cumulative, potent, and lasting effect."[18] The title of his book, *Hollywood vs. America,*[19] gets the point across quite succinctly.

On the formal education side of the ledger, the policy exclusion of the Bible as a standard of moral truth for America's youth in the case of Abington vs. Schempp (1963) rendered the field of moral and character development an ephemeral issue to blow hither and yon with the sands of time, at the whim of every student as he or she should choose...for any reason...at any time...depending upon however one might "feel" at a given moment. The result: "There is absolutely no moral consensus at all in the 1990s. Everyone is making up their own personal moral codes."[20]

Allan Bloom, in his critique of higher education in our nation, *The Closing of the American Mind,* decries the death-blow dealt to our national soul and character. The introductory page facing the title page says it all, "How Higher Education Has Failed Democracy and Impoverished the Souls of Today's Students."[21]

In our supposed "value-neutral" education these past twenty years, we have, in fact, "preached" a new set of values and have subverted the values espoused generally by American society for the previous three hundred years. The result: an *integrity crisis*! And the crisis of integrity has invaded the very citadels of truth and the guardians of moral righteousness—our churches.

A CALL TO CHRISTENDOM

The assault of moral neutrality has laid siege against "America's Only Hope," the Christian church. If it were not for the Scriptures declaring that "the gates of hell shall not prevail"[22] against God's church, one might be even more concerned for the breach of the pillars of truth in Christendom—both Protestant and Roman Catholic.

Situational morality has threatened the moral and spiritual integrity of the Catholic church, resulting in major confrontations among both priest and parishioner on the authority of the Scriptures and their governance in the affairs and personal lives of citizens. This critical and growing confrontation led Pope John Paul II to issue his encyclical entitled "The Splendor of Truth" throughout the Catholic church. With fervor he proclaims that good is clearly distinct from evil, that morality is not situational, that right is right and wrong really is wrong. Only absolute morality, argues the pope, provides the basis for democratic equality of all citizens. Only when people hold to the same standards of good and evil can they be free and equal.[23]

Protestant Americans are likewise confronted with the assault of an increasingly valueless popular culture. *Time* magazine, in the April 5, 1993 issue, presents a cross on its front cover with illustrations revealing the "cross"-roads of American society and declaring, "The Generation That Forgot God." The lead article, "The Church Search," discusses the efforts of the "baby boomer" generation to seek after religion—but on their own terms, "shopping for a custom-made God."[24]

The *Time* article observes, "A growing choir of critics

contends that in doing whatever it takes to lure those fickle customers, churches are at risk of losing their heritage—and their souls."[25] Folks, that means our churches are jeopardizing their integrity! Analysts say mainline Protestant churches have "failed to transmit a compelling Christian message to their own children or to anybody else."[26] The result is that the highest incidence of moral uncertainty is among mainline Protestants, where seventy-three percent do not believe in an absolute truth upon which to guide human behavior.[27]

But evangelical Protestants are also caught in the vice grip of the integrity crisis. Resorting to technology and marketing techniques, concern is mounting that rather than the churches "using some marketing techniques...marketing techniques are beginning to use the church."[28] Evangelicals have followed the suit of their liberal predecessors to placate popular culture. Even among conservatives, warns David Wells in *No Place For Truth,* biblical truth "is being edged out by the small and tawdry interest of the self in itself."[29] The Christian gospel, he says, is becoming "indistinguishable from a host of alternative self-help doctrines."[30] "And in this wilderness, voices crying about a loss of spiritual integrity are not easily heard."[31]

The *Time* article concludes, "Many of those who have rediscovered churchgoing may ultimately be shortchanged, however, if the focus of their faith seems subtly to shift from the glorification of God to the gratification of man."[32] Os Guinness declares in his book that we are "Dining with the Devil" in playing the game of enticement with popular culture.[33] I ask this: If the church won't tell the truth, who will?

Warren Wiersbe, evangelical author and pastor, has lovingly but firmly warned the evangelical community of believers in his book, *The Integrity Crisis.* He states, "Our values are confused. And we're so comfortable in this snare of our own making that we don't really want to get out! The vested interests in the evangelical world are enormous, and revival might cost us financially."[34] He adds a message of hope: "You and I can help to make the difference."[35] Then he warns, "Our greatest danger is that we may waste our opportunity."[36] Wiersbe concludes, "The wrong kind of preachers have created the wrong kind of Christians by declaring the wrong kind of message, compelled by the wrong motives."[37] That, my friends, is an integrity crisis.

America's Only Hope, declares Dr. Tony Evans, is the Christian church. But "instead of setting the agenda for society, the church has been crippled by society." The church is no longer the church in the world; rather, the world is in the church."[38] In unmistakable clarity, Evans points the way to the restoration of integrity in both the nation and the church. "As God's people go, so goes the culture. Until we decide to be His church rather than a group of religious-looking people, our society is hopeless." This means we must "infiltrate the culture with God's righteousness."[39]

To the church, we either is...or we ain't. Let's clean up our act. As de Tocqueville stated a century-and-a-half ago, let our pulpits once again "flame with righteousness," and let our lives demonstrate the same. To appearances, we have enough dirty laundry to keep the Laundromat of God's forgiveness busy for a century. But it's time for us to confess our sins to God and our faults to one another, that we may be healed.

The Lord, the Supreme Ruler of Nations, set His own conditions for revival, renewal, and restoration. He said:

If my people...
will humble themselves,
and pray,
and seek my face,
and turn from their wicked ways;
then [and only then] will I hear from heaven,
and will forgive their sin,
and will heal their land.[40]

That is the condition for real change, folks. America needs a church worthy of the name of the Lord—a church of integrity without spot, or wrinkle, or any such thing. As David of old cried out, "Let integrity and uprightness preserve me."[41]

A NOTE TO MOMS AND DADS

Parents are the most important leaders in the nation. What you do in modeling integrity for your children will determine not only the future of America, but will determine if there will be a "land of the free and a home of the brave." May I leave you with a few helpful suggestions to help you work through the mine fields of moral training as you seek to develop allegiance on the foundation of integrity.

DEVELOPING ALLEGIANCE IN YOUR KIDS

Allegiance is a form of loyalty. If mom and dad are loyal to God and loyal to the principles they profess, the children will likely follow. Like father, like son; like mother, like daughter.

Integrity is the true basis for allegiance. Integrity is behavior consistent with what I say I value. If moms and dads model this consistently within the home, the kids will likely develop allegiance to those values.

Allegiance is a matter of relationship. Our children will develop allegiance to God if they develop a relationship with Him. They will be more prone to develop a relationship if they see it genuinely modeled by mom and dad. In the same way, they are more likely to develop an attitude of respect and allegiance to their country if those attitudes are alive and well in their parents.

Rules without relationship breed rebellion. Rules with relationship breed allegiance.

Relationship depends on integrity for survival. Neither you nor your children will commit to a spouse, a church, or a nation where there is no allegiance. There is no allegiance where there is no relationship, and there can be no relationship where there is no integrity. Integrity is the bottom line, folks. So teach your children well.

THE ENEMY WITHIN

In a May 2, 1992 address in Washington, D.C., Chuck Colson spoke of a "fundamental change in the values of American life" resulting from "a breakdown of character..." He noted that the previous year, ten percent of the U.S. Senate was under investigation, a H.U.D. official was under indictment for skimming, there were 11,050 successful prosecutions of office holders by the Department of Justice, and the president of a major university resigned for multimillion-dollar fraud. These, he said, are the reflections of a "loss of character."

And then Colson notes, "A democracy isn't held together by law. A democracy is held together by shared values—a certain understanding of right and wrong." But "without a moral consensus, there can be no law." And "America will collapse if everyone does what is right in his own eyes."[42]

The enemy is within! No power could do to us what we have done to ourselves. We must restore a moral consensus in our society. The only workable consensus is one based upon the Bible. It is the source from which our forefathers drew their wisdom and from which issued their integrity of life action. Lincoln advised, "...but for the Book we could not know right from wrong."[43] And it was he who said, "This Nation, under God, shall have a new birth of freedom..."[44] That is still true today.

We can talk a "pluralistic" society all we want, but we must look at the fruit of a valueless culture utterly lacking in integrity. The social consequences to date have been horrendous. But we have seen nothing yet as compared to what lies ahead if we do not individually, as families, and as a nation immediately begin an abrupt change of course.

To repeat, our founding president, George Washington, in his farewell address warned, "Let us with caution indulge the supposition that morality can be maintained without religion.... Reason and experience both forbid us to expect that National morality can prevail in exclusion of religious principle."[45] If we would be restored outside, in our society, we must first be restored inside, in our hearts.

Washington, as Commander-in-Chief of the Continental Army, gave the following address before the Battle of Long Island. The words seem strangely appropriate here, although our enemy is within:

> The time is now near at hand which must probably determine whether Americans are to be freemen or slaves.... The fate of unborn millions will now depend, under God, on the courage and conduct of this army. Our cruel and unrelenting enemy leaves us only the choice of brave resistance, or the most abject submission. We have, therefore, to resolve to conquer or to die.[46]

They took the challenge against the enemy without, and God honored their commitment. We have reaped the blessings of their faithful courage to this day. Will our children and grandchildren be able to say the same of our triumphal victory over the advancing enemy within? It's up to you. And it's up to me.

INTEGRITY BEGINS AT HOME

Integrity begins at home, in the little things. It begins with not calling in "sick" to my employer when I want to go shopping. It begins with reporting my untraceable cash income on my tax return. It begins with paying for goods and services I purchase in a timely manner. It begins with the way we run our churches and present God's truth. It begins with truth, the whole truth, and nothing but the truth. It begins with you, and with me.

At its root, the allegiance gap is not a problem with the American spirit but with the spirit of Americans. In 1954, the words *under God* were added to our Pledge of Allegiance by an act of Congress. This was not meant to signal a change in our nation's spiritual direction. Instead, these words were added in order to reflect the essential role God and His Holy Scriptures had played in our national life since the first settlers landed on these shores. But now, in our pride, we seem to have determined we no longer need this "Divine Friend."

In 1962 we officially removed prayer from our schools. The next year we removed the Bible, and our Supreme Court has told us we can't have the Ten Commandments in our schools because the students might read them; and if they read them, they might obey them. And many of us, including some professing Christians, no longer consider the Bible to be authoritative. The Ten Commandments have become the Ten Suggestions. We have turned from being "One nation, under God" into "One nation, under Greed." As the September 1992 issue of *Forbes* magazine warned, "It is a terrible thing when people lose God."[47] And are we not experiencing terrible things? Do we not see the cause-and-effect relationships in every social indication in our beloved nation?

If we would once again pledge our allegiance with conviction of heart, we must once again become men and women of integrity. And—bottom line—our integrity crisis is a spiritual crisis. If I as a father and husband am not "under God" and submitted to His authority, there is no hope for the nation. For the nation is only a mirror of we the people. "Things" will look up when we do.

America has entered its time of reckoning. This is "an hour

of truth that will not be delayed."[48] As we have seen, our real crisis is a "crisis of cultural authority."[49] We must once again choose as did our Founding Fathers. It is a crisis that "goes to the heart of America's character and strength. It is both a sobering time and a time of great opportunity to rebuild. We must resolve our current identity crisis." Who are "we"? As Os Guiness has so aptly said, "At stake is the vision of America that will become America's vision."[50]

May our motto, "In God is our trust," become an undistorted reflection of our national mind and heart. And may God, through your integrity, PRESERVE US A NATION.

CHAPTER SEVENTEEN

Speak Up, Stand Up

AN EDITORIAL IN THE JANUARY 6, 1992 issue of *Newsweek* magazine is entitled, "The Future Be Damned." It is a piercing, if not scathing, observation of the growing propensity of Americans to live for today without caring for tomorrow and the generations to follow. The author concludes, "The real harm that we suffer now is to our national self-esteem. We won't endure small hurts today to avoid larger hurts tomorrow, and we know it. Self-deception has become a way of life."[1]

I pray that will not be America's epitaph. You and I are writing the script of America's future today. With every word, every decision, every thought, every act—for good or ill—we are either rebuilding our foundations or bringing further decay. Each one of us plays a part. We each bear the consequences.

This is the greatest opportunity you have ever had to personally make a difference. I hope you will begin today, if you have not already begun. The seriousness of our nation's dilemma will not permit delay. Every day is critical.

There are those who have set themselves with intent to destroy and undermine the principles which have made America great—those which have allowed the hand of God to prosper us. We must not be deterred. United we will stand, divided we will fall. Together, with God's help, we CAN SAVE

AMERICA. I pray we can count on you. Can we?

If this book has been helpful and of encouragement to you, please write and let me know (the address of Save America is found at the end of the book, immediately following the chapter notes). I know my message has been direct, but the time for "political correctness" and word mincing is long past. A battle is raging for the mind, heart, and soul of America! If you share my concern for our nation, obtain further copies of this book for your friends, relatives, co-workers, pastor, club members, and others. Do not let discouragement tie your hands or close your mouth. It's time to speak up! It's time to *stand up!*

The title of this book came from the second stanza of our national anthem, *The Star Spangled Banner*, written by Francis Scott Key, a godly lawyer. I would like to close with those words:

O thus be it e're,
When free men shall stand;
Between their loved homes
And the war's desolation.
Blessed with victory and peace,
May the heaven rescued land,
Praise the Power that hath made
And preserved us a nation.
Then conquer we must
When our cause it is just,
And this be our motto:
IN GOD IS OUR TRUST
And the Star Spangled Banner
In triumph shall wave
O're the land of the free
And the home of the brave.

May God, through you, Bless America.
Let's *PRESERVE US A NATION!*

Remember these words:

I am only one, but I am one.
I cannot do everything, but I can do something.
What I can do, I should do,
And by the grace of God, I will do.

—Everett Hale

In this hour of crisis:
What I CAN DO is first defined
by what I SHOULD BE!

NOTES

CHAPTER 1—IF I COULD SPEAK

Note: Much of the general information regarding the Statue of Liberty was taken from Sue Burchard, *Birth to Rebirth, Statue of Liberty* (New York: Harcourt Brace Jovanovich, Publishers, 1985).

1. Irving Berlin, "God Bless America."

CHAPTER 2—A NATION AT RISK

1. Gaillard Hunt and James B. Scott, ed., *The Debates in the Federal Convention of 1787 Which Framed the Constitution of the United States of America*, reported by James Madison (New York: Oxford University Press, 1920), pp. 181-182.

2. Attributed to James Madison, known as the Father of the Constitution.

3. Tim LaHaye, *Faith of Our Founding Fathers* (Brentwood, Tenn: Wolgemuth & Hyatt, Publishers Inc., 1987), p. 92.

4. As compiled by James D. Richardson, *Messages and Papers of the Presidents*, 1789-1897, Vol. 1 (Published by Bureau of National Literature 1913, c. 1897), George Washington's Farewell Address, pp. 205-216.

5. Alexis de Tocqueville, *Democracy in America* (first published in 1835 and 1840). *Note*: de Tocqueville arrived in the United States from France in May 1831 and returned to his native France in February 1832 after studying American society and forming his impressions, which have become a classic commentary on the American experiment in self-government and the American people.

6. Robert Flood, *The Rebirth of America* (Philadelphia: The Arthur S. De Moss Foundation, 1986), p. 12.

7. *Messages and Papers of the Presidents*, Vol. 1, pp. 205-216.

8. A Congressional resolution in 1954 ratified by President Dwight D. Eisenhower.

9. Robert J. Samuelson, "How Our American Dream Unraveled," *Newsweek*, March 2, 1992, p. 32-39.

10. Jerry Adler, et al., "Down in the Dumps," *Newsweek*, January 13, 1992, pp. 18-22, with front-cover headline.

11. Samuelson, "How Our American Dream Unraveled," p. 32.

12. Robert Hughes, "The Fraying of America" (*Time*, February 3, 1992), pp. 44-49, with front-cover headline.

13. Bart Ziegler, "Experts denounce Japan's comment on U.S. laziness" (Associated Press), *Star News* (Pasadena, Calif.; January 21, 1992), p. 1.

14. Charles Krauthammer, "In Praise of Mass Hypocrisy," *Time*, April 27, 1992.

15. Samuelson, "How Our American Dream Unraveled," p. 38.

CHAPTER 3—REMEMBERING OUR FOUNDATIONS

1. James D. Richardson, *Messages and Papers of the Presidents* (1789-1897), Vol. VI, p. 164, March 30, 1863.

2. John Adams, *The Works of John Adams*, Charles Francis Adams, ed. (Boston: Little, Brown 1854), Vol. IX, p. 229.

3. James Patterson and Peter Kim, *The Day America Told the Truth* (New York:

Prentice Hall, 1991).

4. Ibid, p. 32.

5. Jefferson, *The Writings of Thomas Jefferson*, Vol. II, p. 227, from Jefferson's "Notes on the State of Virginia," Query XVIII, 1781.

6. Noah Webster, *The History of the United States* (New Haven, Conn.: Durrie & Peck 1832), p. 309.

7. Thomas Jefferson, *Writings of Thomas Jefferson*, Albert Bergh, ed. (Washington D.C.: Thomas Jefferson Memorial Assoc., 1904), Vol. II, p. 227, from "Jefferson's Notes on the State of Virginia," Query XVIII, p. 289, 1781.

8. *The Bible*, Psalm 11:3.

CHAPTER 4—AMERICA'S SEARCH FOR LEADERS

1. James Madison, *The Papers of James Madison*, Robert Rutland, ed. (Chicago: University of Chicago Press, 1973), Vol. VIII, pp. 299,304, June 20, 1785.

2. *The Bible*, Philippians 2:8.

3. Gorton Carruth & Eugene Ehrlich, ed., *American Quotations* (Avenil, N.J.: Wings Books 1992), pp. 461-463, John F. Kennedy Inaugural Address January 20, 1961.

4. A. A. Montapert, ed., *Distilled Wisdom* (Englewood Cliffs, N.J.: Prentice-Hall Inc., 1965), p. 137.

5. Ibid, p. 137.

6. Ibid, p. 137.

7. Charles Krauthammer, "In Praise of Mass Hypocrisy," *Time*, April 27, 1992.

CHAPTER 5—RESTORING THE AMERICAN VISION

1. James Patterson and Peter Kim, *The Day America Told the Truth* (New York: Prentice-Hall Inc., 1991), p. 5.

2. Ibid, p. 6.

3. *The Bible*, Proverbs 29:18.

4. James D. Richardson, *Messages and Papers of the Presidents* (1789-1897) Vol. V (Insert of Abraham Lincoln's "Gettysberg Address" between pp. 3371 and 3372).

5. Daniel L. Marsh, *Unto the Generations* (Buena Park, Calif.: ARC, 1968) p. 51; Tim LaHaye, *Faith of Our Founding Fathers* (Brentwood, Tenn.: Wolgemuth & Hyatt, 1987), p. 48.

6. Peter Marshall and David Manuel, *The Light and the Glory* (Grand Rapids, Mich.: Fleming H. Revell, 1977), p. 31. Quoting Isaiah 49:1, 6 from *The Bible*, Revised Standard Version.

7. Peter Marshall and David Manuel, *The Light and the Glory* (Grand Rapids, Mich.: Fleming Revell, 1977), p. 111.

8. Ibid, p. 120. (From a photograph of the original in Kate Caffrey's *The Mayflower*), p. 115. Also, William Bradford, *The Plymouth Settlement* (Portland, Ore.: American Heritage Ministries, 1988), pp. 75-76.

9. Bradford, Ibid, p. 226; Marshall, Ibid, p. 144.

10. Marshall, Ibid, p. 161-162.

11. Ibid, p. 162.

12. Ibid, p. 185.

13. Robert N. Bellah, et al., *Habits of the Heart* (Regents of the University of

California, 1985; reprinted in 1986 by Harper and Row), pp. 284-285, 303.

14. James D. Richardson, *Messages and Papers of the Presidents* (1789-1897) (Printing authorized by Congress), Vol. 1, Washington's Inaugural Address, p. 44.

15. John F. Schroeder, ed., *Maxims of Washington* (Mt. Vernon, Vir.: Mt. Vernon Ladies Assoc., 1942), p. 287.

16. James D. Richardson, *Messages and Papers of the Presidents*, Vol. 1, p. 212.

17. Ibid, p. 212.

18. Tim LaHaye, *Faith of Our Founding Fathers* (Brentwood, Tenn.: Wolgemuth & Hyatt, 1987), pp. xi-xii.

19. Gaillard Hunt and James B. Scott, ed., *The Debates in the Federal Convention of 1787 Which Framed the Constitution of the United States of America*, reported by James Madison (New York: Oxford Univ. Press, 1920), pp. 181-182.

20. Benjamin Franklin, *The Writings of Benjamin Franklin*, Albert Henry Smyth, ed., 1907 (reprinted New York: Haskell House Publishers, 1970), Vol. IX, 569, from letter on April 17, 1787.

21. John Adams, *The Works of John Adams, Second President of the United States*, Charles Francis Adams, ed. (Boston: Little, Brown, 1854), Vol. IX, p. 229.

22. Thomas Jefferson, *Writings of Thomas Jefferson*, Albert Bergh, ed. (Washington D.C.: Thomas Jefferson Memorial Assoc., 1904), Vol. II, p. 227, from Jefferson's "Notes on the State of Virginia," Query XVIII, p. 289, 1781.

23. James D. Richardson, *Messages and Papers of the Presidents* (1787-1897), Vol. V, "Gettysburg Address" insert between p. 3371 and p. 3372.

24. James W. Michaels, "Oh, Our Aching Angst," *Forbes*, September 14, 1992, p. 54.

25. Peggy Noonan, "You'd Cry Too If It Happened to You," *Forbes*, September 14, 1992, p. 69.

26. Ibid.

27. Ibid.

28. Ibid.

29. Ibid, p. 65.

30. Ibid.

31. Ibid.

CHAPTER 6—A MATTER OF PRINCIPLE

1. Lewis C. Henry, ed., *Five Thousand Quotations for All Occasions* (Garden City, N.Y.: Doubleday and Co., 1945), p. 219.

2. A. A. Montapert, ed., *Distilled Wisdom* (Englewood Cliffs, N.J.: Prentice Hall, Inc., 1964), p. 235.

3. Ibid, p. 259.

4. Ibid.

5. H. Jackson Brown, Jr., *A Father's Book of Wisdom* (Nashville, Tenn.: Rutledge Press, 1988), p. 131.

6. James D. Richardson, *Messages and Papers of the Presidents* (1789-1897) (Printing authorized by Congress), Vol. 1, Washington Inaugural Address, p. 212.

7. John Adams, *The Works of John Adams, Second President of the United States*, Charles Francis Adams, ed. (Boston: Little, Brown 1854), Vol. IX, p. 229.

8. Ibid, p. 229.

9. Nancy Leigh De Moss, ed., *The Rebirth of America* (Philadelphia: Arthur S. De Moss Foundation, 1986), p. 33.

10. Author unknown.

11. H. Jackson Brown, Jr., ed., *A Father's Book of Wisdom* (Nashville, Tenn.: Rutledge Hill Press, 1988), p. 23.

12. Lewis C. Henry, ed., *Five Thousand Quotations for All Occasions*, p. 219.

CHAPTER 7—NOTHING BUT THE TRUTH

1. George Washington, *Maxims of George Washington*, John Frederick Schroeder, ed. (Mount Vernon, Vir.: The Mount Vernon Ladies' Assoc.) 1989, p. 141, from a letter to Alexander Hamilton, August 28, 1788, as taken from "Writings," Vol. 30, p. 67.

2. Paul Gray, "Lies, Lies, Lies," *Time*, October 5, 1992, pp. 32-38.

3. John Barry and Roger Charles, "Sea of Lies," *Newsweek*, July 13, 1992, pp. 29-37.

4. Paul Gray, "Lies, Lies, Lies," *Time*, October 5, 1992, p. 34.

5. Ibid, p. 32.

6. James Patterson and Peter Kim, *The Day America Told the Truth* (New York: Prentice Hall Press, 1991), p. 45.

7. Ibid, p. 49.

8. George Barna, *What Americans Believe—The Barna Report* (Ventura, Calif.: Regal Books, 1991), p. 36.

9. Ibid, p. 83.

10. Ibid.

11. Ibid.

12. Patterson and Kim, *The Day America Told the Truth*, p. 31.

13. *The Bible*, John 18:38.

14. A. A. Montapert, ed., *Distilled Wisdom* (Englewood Cliffs, N.J.: Prentice Hall, Inc., 1964, 1965), p. 201.

15. H. Jackson Brown, Jr., ed., *A Father's Book of Wisdom* (Nashville, Tenn.: Rutledge Hill Press, 1988), p. 62.

16. Peter Marshall and David Manuel, *The Light and the Glory* (Old Tappan, N.J.: Fleming H. Revell Co., 1977) p. 370, note 10.

17. *The Bible*, John 8:31-32, Revised Standard Version.

CHAPTER 8—THE LAMP OF VIRTUE

1. David H. Appel, *An Album for Americans* (New York: Triangle Publications/Crown Publishers, Inc., 1983), p. 87.

2. Alexis de Tocqueville, *Democracy in America*.

3. Gertrude Himmelfarb, "A De-moralized Society," *Forbes*, September 14, 1992, pp. 120-128.

4. Paul Simon, *The Sounds of Silence*.

5. James Patterson and Peter Kim, *The Day America Told the Truth* (New York: Prentice-Hall Press, 1991); excerpts compiled from throughout book.

6. Ibid, p. 238.

7. Ibid, p. 55.

8. Gertrude Himmelfarb, "A De-Moralized Society," *Forbes*, September 14, 1992, p. 128.

9. Ibid.

10. Ibid.

11. A. A. Montapert, ed., *Distilled Wisdom* (Englewood Cliffs, N.J.: Prentice-

Hall, Inc., 1964, 1965), p. 332.

12. Tim La Haye, *Faith of Our Founding Fathers* (Brentwood, Tenn.: Wolgemuth & Hyatt, 1987), p. 91.

13. Ibid., p. 97.

14. Ibid.

15. Ibid.

16. Ibid.

17. Ibid.

18. Nancy Leigh De Moss, ed., *The Rebirth of America* (Philadephia: The Arthur S. De Moss Foundation, 1986), p. 33.

19. Charles Krauthammer, "In Praise of Mass Hypocrisy," *Time*, April 27, 1992, p. 74.

CHAPTER 9—OUR SACRED HONOR

1. A. A. Montapert, ed., *Distilled Wisdom* (Englewood Cliffs, N.J.: Prentice-Hall, Inc., 1964, 1965), p. 201.

2. Nancy Leigh De Moss, ed., *The Rebirth of America* (Philadelphia: Arthur De Moss Foundation, 1986), p. 15.

3. Ibid., pp. 15-16.

4. Ibid, p. 16.

5. Ibid, p. 16.

6. Ibid, p. 24.

7. A. A. Montapert, ed., *Distilled Wisdom*, p. 235.

8. *The Bible*, 1 Samuel 15:22.

9. James Patterson and Peter Kim, *The Day America Told the Truth* (New York: Prentice Hall Press, 1991), p. 56.

10. Ibid, p. 94.

11. Ibid, p. 94.

12. Ibid, p. 95.

13. Ibid, p. 207.

14. Ibid, pp. 207-210.

15. Paul Johnson, "An Awakened Conscience," *Forbes*, September 14, 1992, p. 188.

16. James D. Richardson, ed., *Messages and Papers of the Presidents* (Printing authorized by Congress, 1897), p. 212.

17. Ibid.

18. Nancy Leigh De Moss, ed., *The Rebirth of America*, p. 33.

19. Ibid, p. 37.

20. Ibid.

21. *The Bible*, 1 Samuel 2:30.

22. Lewis C. Henry, ed., *Five Thousand Quotations for All Occasions* (Garden City, N.Y.: Doubleday & Co., Inc., 1945), p. 123.

23. *The Bible*, Proverbs 18:12.

24. Ibid.

25. *The Bible*, 1 Peter 5:6.

26. *The Bible*, Isaiah 60:12.

27. Frank S. Mead, ed., *12,000 Religious Quotations* (Grand Rapids, Mich.: Baker Book House, 1989), p. 391.

28. Ibid.

29. J. C. Penny, *Fifty Years With the Golden Rule* (New York: Harper & Brothers

Publishers, 1950), p. 239.

30. Ibid, p. 242.

31. Ibid, p. 243.

32. Ibid, pp. 244-245.

CHAPTER 10—*SEMPER FI*

1. David H. Appel, ed., *An Album for Americans* (New York: Crown Publishers, Inc., 1983), p. 40.

2. Fred Cook, *The American Revolution* (New York: Golden Press, 1963), pp. 128-130.

3. Lewis C. Henry, ed., *Five Thousand Quotations for All Occasions* (Garden City, N.Y.: Doubleday & Co., Inc., 1945), p. 46.

4. *The Bible*, Song of Solomon 2:15.

5. A. A. Montapert, ed., *Distilled Wisdom* (Englewood Cliffs, N.J.: Prentice-Hall, Inc., 1965), p. 154.

6. Ibid.

7. George Gallup, Jr., *Forecast 2000* (New York: William Morrow and Company, Inc., 1984), p. 113.

8. Ibid, p. 114.

9. Ibid.

10. Ibid, pp. 114-123.

11. James Patterson and Peter Kim, *The Day America Told the Truth* (New York: Prentice Hall Press, 1991), p. 94.

12. Ibid, p. 95.

13. Ibid, p. 100.

14. Ibid, p. 101.

15. *Newsweek*, January 18, 1993 (front cover). Feature article, pp. 16-23.

16. George Barna, *The Future of the American Family* (Chicago: Moody Press, 1993), p. 26.

17. Ibid, p. 27.

18. Ibid, p. 28.

19. Ibid, p. 35.

20. James C. Dobson, *Straight Talk to Men and Their Wives* (Waco, Texas: Word Books, 1980), p. 21.

21. Ibid.

22. Ibid.

23. Ibid, p. 22.

24. Ibid.

25. Ibid (quoting Derek Prince).

26. Author unknown.

27. George Barna, *The Future of the American Family*, p. 110.

28. *The Bible*, Romans 1:21-32 (specifically vs. 30); 2 Timothy 3:1-7 (specifically vs. 2).

29. *The Bible*, Malachi 4:6.

30. A. A. Montapert, ed., *Distilled Wisdom*, p. 117.

31. E. C. McKenzie, ed., *14,000 Quips and Quotes* (Grand Rapids, Mich.: Baker Book House, 1980), pp. 143-144.

32. Gorton Carruth and Eugene Ehrlich, eds., *American Quotations* (New York: Wings Books, 1988), p. 198.

33. Ibid, p. 200.

34. A. A. Montapert, ed., *Distilled Wisdom*, p. 118.

35. *The Bible*, 1 Corinthians 4:2.

36. *The Bible*, Ecclesiastes 12:13.

37. Peter Marshall and David Manuel, *The Light and the Glory* (Old Tappan, N.J.: Fleming H. Revell, 1977), p. 120.

38. Ibid, pp. 161-162.

39. Ibid, p. 162.

40. Anthony T. Evans, *America's Only Hope* (Chicago: Moody Press, 1990), p. 62.

41. Ibid.

42. *The Bible*, 1 Peter 4:17.

43. George Gallup, Jr., *Forecast 2000*, p. 153.

44. Alexis de Tocqueville, *Democracy in America*.

45. Anthony T. Evans, *America's Only Hope*, p. 75.

46. Ibid.

47. Ibid, p. 76.

48. Ibid, p. 77.

49. Ibid, p. 77.

50. Ibid, p. 77.

51. Ibid, p. 77.

52. Ibid, p. 78.

53. Ibid, p. 78.

54. Ibid, p. 78.

55. Peggy Noonan, "You'd Cry Too If It Happened To You," *Forbes*, September 14, 1992, p. 68.

56. Jon Mohr, "Find Us Faithful" (Birdwing Music/Jonathan Mark Music, c. 1987).

CHAPTER 11—TAKE COURAGE

1. David H. Appel, ed., *An Album for Americans* (New York: Triangle Publications, Inc./Crown Publishers, Inc., 1983), p. 40.

2. Ibid, p. 12.

3. Ibid, p. 77.

4. Ibid, p. 102.

5. William Bradford, *Of Plimouth Plantation*, Wright and Potter edition, pp. 34-35.

6. David H. Appel, ed., *An Album for Americans*, p. 33.

7. Ibid, pp. 15-16.

8. Gorton Carruth and Eugene Ehrlich, eds., *American Quotations* (Avenel, New Jersey: Wings Books, 1988), p. 164.

9. Ibid, p. 399.

10. David H. Appel, ed., *An Album for Americans*, p. 74.

11. James Patterson and Peter Kim, *The Day America Told the Truth* (New York: Prentice Hall Press, 1991), p. 25.

12. Richard Halverson, *Perspective*, April 22, 1992.

13. Patterson and Kim, *The Day America Told the Truth*, p. 28.

14. Ibid.

15. Ibid, p. 32.

16. A. A. Montapert, ed., *Distilled Wisdom* (Englewood Cliffs, N.J.: Prentice Hall, Inc., 1964), p. 80.

17. James Michaels, "Oh, Our Aching Angst," *Forbes*, September 14, 1992, p. 54.

18. A. A. Montapert, ed., *Distilled Wisdom*, p. 74.

19. Lewis C. Henry, ed., *Five Thousand Quotations for All Occasions* (Garden City, N.Y.: Doubleday & Company, Inc., 1945), p. 49.

20. William Bentley Bell, ed., *In Search of a National Morality* (Grand Rapids, Mich.: Baker Book House, 1992), p. 12.

21. Ibid, p. 43.

22. Saxe Cummings, ed., *The Basic Writings of George Washington* (New York: Random House, 1948), p. 637.

23. Abraham Lincoln, "The Gettysburg Address."

24. Nancy Leigh De Moss, ed., *The Rebirth of America* (Philadelphia: The Arthur S. De Moss Foundation, 1986), p. 16.

25. A. A. Montapert, ed., *Distilled Wisdom*, p. 80.

26. Ibid.

27. E. C. McKenzie, ed., *14,000 Quips & Quotes* (Grand Rapids, Mich.: Baker Book House, 1980), p. 114.

28. Ibid.

29. *The Bible*, Luke 18:1.

30. A. A. Montapert, ed., *Distilled Wisdom*, p. 80.

31. *The Bible*, Joshua 1:8,9.

CHAPTER 12—FAITH AND FREEDOM

1. Fred Cook, *The American Revolution* (New York: Golden Press, 1963), p. 105.

2. *The Story of America* (Pleasantville, N.Y.: The Reader's Digest Assoc., Inc., 1975), p. 36.

3. David H. WP, ed., *An Album for Americans* (New York: Triangle Publications/Crown Publishers, 1983), p. 43.

4. Gorton Carruth and Eugene Ehrlich, eds., *American Quotations* (Avenil, N.J.: Wings Books, 1988), p. 583.

5. John Frederick Schroeder, ed., *Maxims of George Washington* (Mount Vernon, Vir.: The Mount Vernon Ladies' Assoc., 1989), p. 202.

6. Ibid, p. 203.

7. James Richardson, ed., *Messages and Papers of the Presidents* (Printing authorized by Congress, ©1897), p. 44.

8. Charles Colson, *The Body* (Dallas: Word Publishing, 1992), p. 41.

9. George Barna, *What Americans Believe* (Ventura, Calif.: Regal Books, 1991), p. 176.

10. Ibid, p. 77.

11. Ibid, p. 179.

12. James Patterson and Peter Kim, *The Day America Told the Truth* (New York: Prentice Hall Press, 1991), p. 199.

13. Ibid, p. 199.

14. Nancy Leigh De Moss, ed., *The Rebirth of America* (Philadelphia: The Arthur S. De Moss Foundation, 1986), p. 32.

15. George Barna, *What Americans Believe*, p. 36.

16. Patterson and Kim, *The Day America Told the Truth*, p. 3.

17. Ibid, pp. 31-32.

18. *Time*, January 13, 1992, p. 34.

19. *Newsweek*, January 13, 1992, front cover and p. 18.

20. *Newsweek*, March 2, 1992, p. 32.

21. *The Bible*, John 8:31,32.

22. William Bradford, *The Plymouth Settlement* (Portland, Ore.: American Heritage Ministries, 1988), pp. 75-76.

23. Alexis de Tocqueville, *Democracy in America*.

24. George Gallup, Jr., *Forecast 2000* (New York: William Morrow and Company, Inc., 1984), p. 151.

25. Ibid, p. 153.

26. Richard N. Ostling, "The Church Search," *Time*, April 5, 1993, p. 46.

27. Ibid, p. 47.

28. Ibid, p. 48.

29. Ibid, p. 48.

30. Ibid.

31. Ibid, p. 49.

32. Nancy Leigh De Moss, ed., *The Rebirth of America*, p. 32.

33. Patterson and Kim, *The Day America Told the Truth*, p. 201.

34. Ibid.

35. Ibid.

36. Ibid, p. 202.

37. Ibid.

38. Ibid.

39. Ibid.

40. *The Bible*, Acts 16:30,31.

41. Katherine Lee Bates, "America the Beautiful."

CHAPTER 13—MY BROTHER'S KEEPER

1. David H. Appel, *An Album for Americans* (New York: Triangle Publications, Inc., 1983), p. 13.

2. Tim La Haye, *Faith of Our Founding Fathers* (Brentwood, Tenn.: Wolgemuth & Hyatt Publishers, Inc., 1987), p. 188.

3. Ibid.

4. Dumas Malone, *The Story of the Declaration of Independence* (New York: Oxford University Press, 1954), p. 109.

5. Robert Flood, *America, God Shed His Grace on Thee* (Chicago: The Moody Bible Institute, 1975), p. 62.

6. Ibid, p. 63.

7. Dumas Malone, *The Story of the Declaration of Independence*, pp. 109-111.

8. Ibid, p. 109.

9. Ibid, pp. 110-111.

10. David H. Appel, *An Album for Americans*, p. 61.

11. *The Bible*, Philippians 2:7.

12. *The Bible*, Matthew 20:27.

13. Gorton Carruth and Eugene Ehrlich, *American Quotations* (Avenil, New Jersey: Wings Books, 1988), p. 583.

14. James Thomas Flexner, *Washington* (Boston: Little, Brown and Company, 1974), p. 214 (from letter to Henry Knox, April 1, 1789).

15. Gorton Carruth and Eugene Ehrlich, *American Quotations*, p. 586 (from a letter to Benjamin Lincoln, October 26, 1788).

16. James Thomas Flexner, *Washington*, p. 214.

17. Robert N. Bellah, et al., *Habits of the Heart* (New York: Harper and Row, 1985), p. 28 (from *Democracy in America*).

18. Peter Marshall and David Manuel, *The Light and the Glory* (Old Tappan,

N.J.: Fleming H. Revell, 1977), p. 161-162.
19. Ibid, p. 157.
20. *Winthrop Papers*, (Massachusetts Historical Society) Vol. I, pp. 196, 201.
21. Robert N. Bellah, et al., *Habits of the Heart*, p. 29.
22. Ibid, p. 28.
23. Ibid, p. 37.
24. Ibid.
25. Ibid.
26. Ibid.
27. Ibid, p. 31.
28. Ibid.
29. *The Bible*, Genesis 4:9.
30. Anthony T. Evans, *America's Only Hope* (Chicago: Moody Press, 1990).
31. Robert N. Bellah, et al., *Habits of the Heart*, p. 303.
32. Ibid.
33. Ibid, p. 223.
34. Anthony T. Evans, *America's Only Hope*, p. 42.
35. Ibid, p. 36.
36. *The Bible*, Matthew 22:37,39.

CHAPTER 14—COMPASSION THAT COUNTS

1. *The Bible*, 2 Timothy 1:7.
2. Gorton Carruth and Eugene Ehrlich, *American Quotations* (Avenil, New Jersey: Wings Books, 1988), p. 179.
3. Ibid, p. 185, from *Democracy in America*.
4. Steven Waldman, "Ask Not—'90's Style," *Newsweek*, September 20, 1993, p. 46.
5. Peter Marshall and David Manuel, *The Light and the Glory* (Old Tappan, N.J.: Fleming H. Revell, 1977), p. 162.
6. Brian Heckmann.
7. John Dawson.
8. Bob Hunt.
9. Dr. John Perkins.
10. Debra Cruel.
11. Charles Colson.
12. Virgil Gulker.

CHAPTER 15—A CIVIL BODY POLITIC

1. Peter Marshall and David Manuel, *The Light and the Glory* (Old Tappan, N.J.: Fleming H. Revell, 1977), p. 120.
2. Ibid, (The Mayflower Compact).
3. Gorton Carruth and Eugene Ehrlich, *American Quotations* (Avenil, New Jersey: Wings Books, 1988), p. 183. Quoting James Russell Lowell in "New England Two Centuries Ago," *Among My Books*, 1870.
4. Peter Marshall, et al., *The Light and the Glory*, pp. 161-164, 180.
5. Tim La Haye, *Faith of Our Founding Fathers* (Brentwood, Tenn.: Wolgemuth & Hyatt Publishers, Inc., 1987), pp. 123-124.
6. Francis Scott Key, "The Star Spangled Banner" (second stanza).
7. *The Bible*, 2 Chronicles 7:14.

8. *The Bible*, 1 Peter 4:17.

9. James D. Richardson, ed., *Messages and Papers of the Presidents* (Publication authorized by Congress, 1897), p. 212.

10. Adams, *The Works of John Adams*, Vol, IX, p. 229.

11. *The Bible*, Deuteronomy 30:19,20.

12. Nancy Leigh De Moss, ed., *The Rebirth of America* (Philadelphia: The Arthur S. De Moss Foundation, 1986), p. 32.

13. *The Bible*, Joshua 24:15.

14. David Barton, *The Myth of Separation* (Aledo, Tex.: Wall Builders Press, 1992), p. 246.

15. Dumas Malone, *The Story of the Declaration of Independence* (New York: Oxford University Press, 1954), p. 78.

16. David Barton, *The Myth of Separation*, pp. 41-46.

17. Marlin Maddoux, *A Christian Agenda* (Dallas: International Christian Media, 1993), p 63.

18. Ibid.

19. Ibid.

20. Ibid, p. 64.

21. *The Bible*, Isaiah 59:1-4.

22. *The Bible*, Isaiah 59:2.

23. *The Bible*, Ephesians 5:27.

24. *The Bible*, Acts 2:1.

25. Alexis de Tocqueville, *Democracy in America*.

CHAPTER 16—THE INTEGRITY GAP

1. David H. Appel, ed., *An Album for Americans* (New York: Triangle Publications, Inc., 1983), p. 252.

2. Carroll C. Calkins, ed., *The Story of America* (Pleasantville, N.Y.: The Reader's Digest Assoc., 1975), p. 49.

3. Eloise Salholz, et al., "Caught in the Act," *Newsweek*, March 23, 1992.

4. Eleanor Cliff, "Running Against the Past," *Newsweek*, April 13, 1992, p. 30. George V. Church, "Questions, Questions, Questions," *Time*, April 20, 1992, p. 38.

5. Gorton Carruth and Eugene Ehrlich, *American Quotations* (Avenil, New Jersey: Wings Books, 1988), p. 52 (from *The Autobiography of Will Rogers*, 1949).

6. Ibid, p. 47. From the First Inaugural Address of Dwight D. Eisenhower, January 20, 1953.

7. Charles Krauthammer, "In Praise of Mass Hypocrisy," *Time*, April 27, 1992, p. 74.

8. George Barna, *The Barna Report—Absolute Confusion* (Ventura, Calif.: Regal Books, 1993).

9. James Patterson and Peter Kim, *The Day America Told the Truth* (New York: Prentice Hall Press, 1991), p. 8.

10. Cal Thomas, *The Death of Ethics in America* (Dallas: Word Publishing, 1988), p. 20.

11. Ibid, p. 21.

12. Ibid, pp. 33-34.

13. Clyde M. Narramore, "Character: Public or Private," *Psychology for Living*, July-August 1992, p. 2.

14. Reference unavailable

15. Reference unavailable

16. Reference unavailable

17. Peggy Noonan, "You'd Cry Too If It Happened to You," *Forbes*, September 14, 1992, p. 69.

18. Michael Medved, "Hollywood's Poison Factory—Making It The Dream Factory Again," *Imprimis*, published by Hillsdale College, Hillsdale, Mich., November 1992, Vol. 21, No. 11.

19. Michael Medved, *Hollywood vs. America* (San Francisco: Harper Collins/Zondervan, 1992).

20. Patterson and Kim, *The Day America Told the Truth*, p. 25.

21. Allan Bloom, *The Closing of the American Mind* (New York: Simon & Schuster, Inc., 1987).

22. *The Bible*, Matthew 16:18.

23. Richard N. Ostling, "A Refinement of Evil," *Time*, October 4, 1993, p. 75.

24. Richard N. Ostling, "The Church Search," *Time*, pp. 44-48.

25. Ibid, p. 46.

26. Ibid, p. 47.

27. George Barna, *What Americans Believe* (Ventura, Calif.: Regal Books, 1991), p. 36.

28. Richard N. Ostling, "The Church Search," p. 48.

29. Ibid, p. 48.

30. David F. Wells, *No Place For Truth* (Grand Rapids, Mich.: Eerdmans Publishing Co., 1993), p. 300.

31. Ibid, p. 295.

32. Richard N. Ostling, "The Church Search," p. 49.

33. Os Guiness, *Dining With the Devil* (Grand Rapids, Mich.: Baker Book House, 1993).

34. Warren W. Wiersbe, *The Integrity Crisis* (Nashville, Tenn.: Thomas Nelson Publishers, 1991), p. 134.

35. Ibid, p. 136.

36. Ibid, p. 135.

37. Ibid, p. 61.

38. Anthony T. Evans, *America's Only Hope* (Chicago: Moody Press, 1990), p. 42.

39. Ibid, p. 39.

40. *The Bible*, 2 Chronicles 7:14.

41. *The Bible*, Psalm 25:21.

42. Chuck Colson, "Challenge To a Vital Faith," *The War Cry* (published by the Salvation Army), July 4, 1992, pp. 4,5,6.

43. Nancy Leigh De Moss, ed., *The Rebirth of America* (Philadelphia: The Arthur S. De Moss Foundation, 1986), p. 37.

44. Ibid, p. 69, from the "Gettysburg Address."

45. James D. Richardson, ed., *Messages and Papers of the Presidents*, p. 212.

46. Carruth and Ehrlich, eds., *American Quotations*, p. 65.

47. Peggy Noonan, "You'd Cry Too If It Happened To You," *Forbes*, September 14, 1992, p. 65.

48. Os Guiness, *The American Hour* (New York: The Free Press, 1993), p. 4.

49. Ibid.

50. Ibid, p. 49.

CHAPTER 17—SPEAK UP, STAND UP

1. Robert J. Samuelson, "The Future Be Damned," *Newsweek*, January 16, 1992, p. 36.

ABOUT THE AUTHOR

Charles Crismier III, founder and president of SAVE AMERICA, and author of this book, brings a unique background to the forefront of our national identity crisis. A husband for twenty-seven years and father of three, Chuck began his career as a public school teacher after graduating summa cum laude from Azusa Pacific University. He received his Juris Doctor in 1974 and established a law practice in Pasadena, California.

Chuck, twice a candidate for the California State Legislature, has been voted president and board member of numerous community organizations and institutions, including his alma mater. In 1993 he was honored with the George Washington Medal of Honor by the Freedom Foundation of Valley Forge, Pennsylvania.

For nearly two decades, Chuck has communicated his vision for spiritual growth and principled living as the keynote speaker of men's retreats, service clubs, marriage enrichment seminars, church conventions, and community gatherings. Having enjoyed success in southern California and having sensed the urgency of this critical hour in America, he was compelled to bring his message to national attention.

In the Summer of 1993, he moved his family to Richmond, Virginia—the birthplace of America—to awaken the national conscience to the covenant between God and the Founding Fathers of our nation. Lost to this generation is the astounding compact made between God and the early settlers that has been edited from our textbooks and the lives of the American people. Groping for direction, our country has lost sight of her purpose and continues to seek leadership from a bankrupt society.

RADIO

Charles Crismier is currently in the process of launching a nationally syndicated daily radio broadcast to "massage" the cutting-edge issues of our times through the grid of moral and spiritual values. A prospectus has been prepared and meetings have been held with the country's largest Christian radio network.

SAVE AMERICA

SAVE AMERICA is a non-profit organization formed by the author in July 1992 as a vehicle for communicating both to the church and to the nation, turning the tide of moral and spiritual values in the land. The commitment is to restore a vision for America and particularly for the Body of Christ within the nation. The organization is dedicated to "renew moral and spiritual values that will restore national vision and purpose." The Board recently adopted the phrase, "A Voice to the Church, a Vision for the Nation" to express the essential focus and the broader base of the ministry's efforts. As a nation, we have lost our way because we have lost our vision.

SAVE AMERICA seeks to reacquaint this generation with the covenant vision responsible for America's greatness—the only hope for restoration of her leadership in the twenty-first century. The key is not political activism, but a decision to join in restoring the spiritual foundations of our national heritage. The unacceptable alternative is to continue to live by the frailties of the human spirit, having defaulted on the covenant which promised life, liberty, and the pursuit of happiness.

OTHER BOOKS

Restoring Racial Unity—Chuck Crismier has recently begun a new book speaking to the issue of racial unity, particularly within the Christian churches of America. Racial accord is perhaps the single greatest challenge to the church in the next decade. In fact, Chuck believes the willingness of God's people to grapple meaningfully with this issue is, if not a pre-condition, a co-extensive condition of the revival so earnestly sought in Christendom. That is a strong statement coming from a conservative, white author, but he is convinced of its truth. SAVE AMERICA is also considering this as a video "special" project.

Hospitality—Chuck Crismier and his wife, Kathie, have already outlined a book which they believe will have tremendous impact in the heart of the Church in America. They have spoken on this subject extensively and believe it to be a cutting-edge subject, foundational to the renewal and restoration of the church. It is the heart out of which God will speak through the church to "touch" a society that is fractured from broken relationships, brash individualism, and breach of covenant commitment. These principles revolutionized and revived the flock they have pastored, as volunteer pastors, and will give restored meaning, purpose, and direction to ministry for both the cloth and the congregation.